ANCHOR BOOKS
PURE POETRY

Edited by

Suzy Goodall

First published in Great Britain in 1997 by
ANCHOR BOOKS
1-2 Wainman Road, Woodston,
Peterborough, PE2 7BU

All Rights Reserved

Copyright Contributors 1996

HB ISBN 1 85930 416 8
SB ISBN 1 85930 411 7

Foreword

Anchor Books is a small press, established in 1992, with the aim of promoting readable poetry to as wide an audience as possible.

We hope to establish an outlet for writers of poetry who may have struggled to see their work in print.

The poems presented here have been selected from many entries. Editing proved to be a difficult and daunting task and as the Editor, the final selection was mine.

This anthology is a collection of poems written entirely by closet poets who may have written poetry to pass time or to express their innermost feelings and thought. Yet they had never shared their verse with others . . . until now. This varied collection brings together an assortment of exciting and fresh poetry never before seen, tasted and appreciated. Pure Poetry.

I trust this selection will delight and please the authors and all those who enjoy reading poetry.

Suzy Goodall
Editor

CONTENTS

Wallet Snaps	E Arnold	1
Untitled	Michael R Jackson	1
Reunion	Mark Newson	2
Inner City Blues	Jonathan Wood	3
Everlasting Peace	Frances Meenan	4
Your Night, My Day	James Nimmo	5
My Father Warned Me	Paul Yussarian	5
Until The Next Time . . .	Jill Myers	6
Take Summer	Peggy Parfitt-Moule	6
Thoughts	Saleh Chaudhri	7
Survival	Jean Drummond	7
Isle Of You	Scott H Mitchell	8
Summer To Fall	Samantha Allen	9
Warning	Sally Brighten	9
My Life	Mabel Josephine Harrison	10
Me Trousers	S J McCluskie	10
Life's Bumpy Road	James Stuart Denby	11
An Isolated Moment	Lesley Jane Grimes	11
The Effect	Caroline Mitchell	12
The Navigator's Lantern	Douglas Boswell	13
Gossip Mongers	E Dibb	13
Shadows	Shân Ellis	14
Untitled	A Rowlands	14
Rebecca	J Robinson	15
Untitled	Brenda Schubert	16
All Alone	Gayle L Norcross	16
School Days	A C Churcher	17
Bygone Days Of Old	Charles Smethurst	18
Our Dream	Louise Ann Jolliffe	19
The Tree	Julia Boyle	20
Child	M Bartley	20
Moonlight	C J Toyne	21
Fear	Lynne Browne	22
The Chase	Chris Lee	23
Echo Mountain	Barbara Dennerly	23
Addiction	M Wojtaszek	24
My Grandson	Eileen Whiston	24

Sunrise Over Castletown Harbour	Julie Ann Sloan	25
A Bright October Day	James Gold	26
Untitled	Mark Anderson	27
Of Weather And Sanity	M B Tildesley	28
Dreamland	P Simpson	28
A Good Life	Janise Murrie	29
Wild Thing	Bill Craggs	30
The Come-Back Cat	Johanna S Emeney	31
Time And The Tide	Helen Wheeler	32
Desire	J D Hart	32
Healthy Life	B Marshall	33
Hardly Help	John Harkin	34
Final Passion	C R Spillett	34
My Grandad	J E Madlin	35
Life	J Baybutt	36
In Love	R M Hancock	36
Rainbows	Ros Silom	37
As I Walked On Through The Stormy Waters	Elizabeth Hall	38
Always Alone	Gemma Bodsworth	38
I Once Heard The Wind	Matthew John Leeming	39
Lost	Tanya Lloyd	39
With Your Love	J M	40
On My Mind	Jane E Hughes	40
Miranda	Linda Swain	41
Senior Citizen - 1996	E A Healy	42
True Horizon	Dona Packman	42
Vigil	Helen Bales	43
Dolphins	Eleanor Harris	44
Living In The Silent World	Amanda Rae Blair	44
A Daughter's Love	Patricia Parker	45
November Morning	Stephen L Cleary	45
Son	Annette Walker	46
I Need A Hug	Barbara Sherlow	47
The Window View	Justin Buckley	48
Green Paint	Chris Roland	48
The Short Cut	D M T Moore	49

A Child's Legacy	Jez Ellison	50
A Furry Tale	Barbara Welsby	50
Black Roses	Emma Satchell	51
Christmas Day	A R Thompson	52
End Of Marriage	Barbara S Maclean	53
Highland Dream	Victoria Helen Turner	54
Beach House	Jayne Edney	54
Unceasing Deceased Unsung	Rebecca Thomson	55
Infatuation	Gillian Mesce	56
With Reference To A Female Gardener . . .	Alan Curtis	57
Death Of A Sparrow	Maude A Ryder	57
The Last Goodbye	Cheryl Morley	58
The Wayward Son	Angela O'Neill	59
No Future	Richard Wolfendale	60
Give An Ear	Olive M Cork	60
Fairy Land	E J Sherwood	61
Tired Old Town	Peter Harris	62
A New Life	Lynn Harvey	62
Her An His Dreams	D Turner	63
Time Transcends Us	Gillian Lindsay	64
Tunnel Of Love	Kelly Souten	64
Birds	Marie Sullivan	65
Make That Special Friend	Trina S Brown	66
Hurst Castle	Doreen J Quilter	66
Sunday	Mary Gilhooly	67
Remembrance	Darryl Williams	68
War Cries	Ian Robertson	68
Soul Analysis	Maria Teresa Reed	69
Dreams	Elaine Tamblyn	70
Respect . . .	J J Connolly	70
Through A Child's Eyes	Karann Bamber	71
Gulp, Gulp	Su Kendall	72
Forever With Me	Emma Louise Nyman	73
The Opinions Of One	Paddy Berry	74
A Day In The Country	T Shutt	75
Poetess	Avril Ellison	76
Cold Night	Sylvia Arthurs	76

The Afterglow	V Wilson	77
Memories	Ethel Cheetham	78
Ice Queen	Evelyn James	79
Epitaph For Rosemary	K Bellamy	80
My England, My Rose	Lindsey Holliday	80
Searching	S Bradbury	81
Dunblane	Irene Dodd	82
All Alone	G Wells	82
Mother Earth	Richard Kirchin	83
Revelation	Graham R Bell	84
Goodbye My Love	Heidi Chalfont	84
The Bookmark	Margaret Scott	85
The Destroyer	Emma Boolaky	86
Searching	N Coleman	86
Power Of One	Kathryn Louise Jordin	87
The Sunset	J Lawson	88
A Plea	Sandra M Leggat	88
House On The Hill	Helena Strauss	89
Past Time	Emily Sissons	90
A Shedded Tear	J Macleod	90
My Private Hell	Nicola Watton	91
Travel Broadens The Heart	Tina Lipman	92
O Death (Life Before Death)	Paul Colbourne	93
Feelings And Thoughts	E Banks	94
Millennium's End	Chris Goodrum	94
Nan	Gill Hewett	95
Looking Across To The Island	Rosie Webster	96
Life Goes On	Susan Hansen	96
Autumn	Linda Tongue	97
Joy Of Conversation	C Baxter	98
Life Of Dreams	E Robson	98
Long Days	Ina Howes	99
Never We See	R J Fowler	100
You're Not A Victim You're A Survivor	June Hierons	101
Carousel	E A Heywood	101

Tuesday Midnight - Cuddleometer On Full ...	Garth	102
Stereotypes	Alison Tilley	103
Hidden Depths!	Freda F Ringrose	103
In Twenties Kent	William G Hackney	104
Fickle Emotions	Christine Barrow	104
A Special Someone	Margaret Ford	105
Yorkshire Heritage	Geoff Bowden	106
Precious Moments	V M Coote	107
Mother	Margaret McQuilton-Morgan	108
Where	Angela Morton	108
Golden Years	Iris Ruthven	109
Mountains	N B Mason	110
Dreams	Peter Fowler	110
The Sunset	Kate Hewitt	111
Message	Gary Stewart	112
Tranquillity	D Mary Cross	112
No Time To Say Goodbye	Doreen Conway-Haynes	113
Death And War	Helen Jackson	114
A Missing Light	Julie Ovington	115
How I feel	Amy Carrigan	115
A Whispered Caress	Hilda Hindle	116
I Saw The Mermaid Burn	Lloyd Richards	116
The Separation	Tracy Roberts	117
Futility	Pauline Hill	117
The Orchard	Kevin Hard	118
1919	F Jensen	119
Through My Window	L Corke	119
To The Dearest Of The Dear	Francis Dias	120
Meteorite Delight	Adrian Stafford	121
Wintertide	Michael Monaghan	122
Rebirth	Doreen H M Scott	122
More Bad News	John E Shepherd	123
Clouds Over Africa	J M Wallace	124
The Storm	B Gibson	124
The Stargazer	Lisa Thompson	125
Her Spirit Has Flown	C M Brackley	125
I'm Out Of Work	William Miller	126

What Is Life Really Worth?	J Muttock	127
The Picture In My Mind . . .	Jeff Chick	128
Love	Fern Hughes	128
A Message To The World	Ronald Elgar	129
Generation Games	K H McGeeney	130
Autumnal Walk	I Blaseby	130
The Youth	Michael C Eames	131
Free In Life	Elizabeth Shaw	132
Darker Days	Nora Yeomans	132
Why?	Katie Ferrier	133
My Friend, Jodie	M Howarth	134
Death Of A Tree (London)	V J M Chadwick	135
The Good Old Days	J D Southall	136
Far	Torrin Clark	136
Cupboard Love	Dorothy Biggins	137
The Dancing Leaves	Elizabeth Eragat	138
The Butterfly	Lisa Taylor	139
Looking Back	Suzanne Hughes	139
Winter	Kate Davies	140
Wrong Times	J W Cash	140
Macbeth And I	Mary Chester-Kadwell	141
Thoughts Of A Year	Maureen Richardson	142
Thoughts During A Hangover	Steve Cooke	143
Love In All Weather	Joan Lister	144
Just Do It!	Neil Gibson	145
The Pedlar Of Shadows	Dorothy Beaumont	146
Roots Of Gold	Les Lambert	146
The End Of Life	S L Smith	147
False Hope	Elizabeth Leach	148
Inna City Blues	Prince Nugent	148
Forlorn	George Parr	149
False Arrest	Marilyn Boil	150
Getting In The Swim Of Things	J Atkin	151
Automation	Laura O'Halloran	152
For Nichola	S J Alexander	153
Lauren	Julie Bolam	154
Mother	Gavin Dodds	154

Young Tom	Linda Bitvus	155
A November Walk	Muriel Roe	156
Forecasting Rain	M Remblance	156
Eyes Of Mine	Anita Craig	157
At Hampton Court	Margaret Turner	158
Durham (Dunholme)	K Porritt	159
Peevish Women	James Coneys	160
Lonely And Old	Karen Brown	161
Why Are You Back?	Sandra Marie Turner	162
Rowth 'O Rhymes With Rodents	Edward Graham Macfarlane	163
Nostalgia	V A Tunstall	164
Business And Money	David H Graham	164
Time	Estelle	165
Freedom	Sam Williams	166
Life's Problems	D J Dodd	166
Desert Depression	Harry Cawood	167
I Wonder Who This Person Is?	Mary Butler	168
War	J A Stewart	168
Slainte	Martin Byrne	169
Mortal News	Grainne McMenamin	170
Trapped	J M Stones	170
My Friend	D M Chatwin	171
The Gardens Of My Past	Norman Watt	172
The Tramp	Carol Graham	173
The Long Long Road	Annette Patricia Williamson	174
Poltergeist	Charles Harry Butler	175
A Seaside Resort In Winter	John R Greene	176
Love's Spirit	Mark Triance	177
A Peaceful Time	K L Wellington	177
The Peace Of Nature	Ann Willow Packwood	178
The Way (Searching Ends)	D J Cox	178
You Laughed At My Tears	D N Gibson	179
Stay	Lorraine Tellis	180
Bonfire Night	C Ormrod	181
Abstract Servitude	Mark Cope	182
My Dream	J Vaughan	182

Closed Minds	Janice M Shaw	183
Another New First	Christine Saunders	184
Peace At War	John Clarke	184
'96	Tommy Carr	185
Let Loose The Ties	Myra Christie	186
The Rose Garden	Brenda Munday	186
The Tramp	M Wain	187
Life With Fear	Louise Reynolds	188
Anguish	Kevin Smith	189
Easter	Francis A Scollin	189
Feigned Magic Of The Fair	Zita Stockbridge	190
Exbridge	Dean Smirthwaite	190
Weston, My Home	R Ellis	191
The Sharing Need	N Phillip	192
Leaving Home	S E Hutchings	193
Would It Were Only The Leaves That Are Dying	John A Gilroy	194
Poison	Emma Brackenbury	194
The Future	Heather Clark	195
The Lights Of Home	Bob Storm	196
Pollution Alley	J J D Selby	196
Thousands Are Still Asleep	Myra Canning	197
The Night Show	Penny Rose	198
Touch	D M Clancy	198
Seduction	J Wilde	199
Life's Journey	Amanda S Holland	200
Found And Lost	David N Grufferty	200
Oasis	Doreen Fiol	201
A Sterling Race	Clare Woodward	202
Nature	Mary Porter	202
Dusk And Dawn	Soma Ghosh	203
War Child	W T J Saward	204
High Me From The Real World	Derry Wootton	204
The Moon	Fiona Fuller	205
Just My Jean	G W Goodban	206
Charlotte	Marlene Tapscott	206

Edward Thomas -		
A Letter Home	Dorothy Ireland	207
Longing	Ken Jones	208
Slow-Time Cafe	Richard B Sharples	209
Who Am I?	Gill Price	210
Mystic Lover	Irene Carss	210
Dad	T J Lucas	211
The School Register		
Of The Thirties	E Monaghan	212
My Friend	Norman Rayne	213
Untitled	Lesley Marie Hewett	214
Sky	Richard Dawson	214
Untitled	L K Tiplady	215
The Lake	Paul Warwick	216
Like Someone In Love . . .	Alistair Chattaway	217
No Laughing Matter	T P Bradley	218
Untitled	A Sander	219
You Must Contain		
The Foundations	Shane Jason	220
My Dream	D Hoyle	221
Judgement Day	Gurdeep Mattu	222
The Treasure Of County Down	Joan Lampard	223
Springtime	Rodger Nuttall	224
This Life	Jean Platt	224
Culloden Moor . . .	Andrew Usher	225
Husband To Wife	Johanna S Emeney	226
Conscience	Susie Crozier	227
Memories	C Worthington	228
His Words	Darren Sidney	229

WALLET SNAPS

It was your soul I saw shining through
Those innocent little girls' eyes:
A reflection, a copy, a product of you
Yet to be taught, yet to grow wise
To the way of life; the pain; the lies.

I can see your soul behind that smile
So pure; so naive; so perfectly new,
To explore the trivial - untrivial trial
Of love versus lust, naked and true.
Will she blossom into a version of you?

I could not rip that rose from her soft little cheek
By taking such soul from her heart.
Without her, your world would be weak
You told me this right from the start:
She is you; you are her; each nothing apart.

It was you in that picture, that came shining through:
Her eyes a reflection, a perfection of you.

E Arnold

UNTITLED

On a windswept headland she stands alone
But for her awe and presence
The sun picks over her shiny eyes, that release this woman's essence
The wind, it howls around her form, who knows what joys await her
What mysteries are there to find, by someone who must take her
She goes inside, the fire is bright, the room is warm
The wind and sun have vanished
I see her now for what she is - a woman to be loved not tarnished.

Michael R Jackson

REUNION

Angels float in the sky
And watch over you and I
Watching over us from above
Sending down their special love

Once they were like us down here
Living their lives of hope and fear.
Now they drift with peace of mind
Now they've left our world behind

Somewhere up there an angel looks down
Keeping an eye on someone dear
Trying to guide her through the burden of life
Fear not little one, your angel is near.

She hears all you say
And sees all you do
Going through your weary day
At night she watches you too.

She's sad you are unhappy
And tries to tell you so
She tries to tell you that she loves you
But this you already know.

One day you'll be together again
Just like you used to be
But until that day you have to wait
For the day when you are free.

When the time is right, don't worry
She'll be with you, forever near
She'll hold your hand and whisper
'Now, your time is here.'

You'll close your eyes and die in peace
And the soul from your body will sever.
And once again on that special day
You'll be with your angel forever.

Mark Newson

INNER CITY BLUES

Born to the beat of a thousand feet,
As they tramp their way through this rainy day,
To the thump of exhausts, that thundering force
That belches forth the fires that scorch
This dusty sphere we tread with our peers,
As we sit at the bar drinking beers as someone else's end draws near.
But who? Is it me or is it you?
Strange to think that every piece of paper that you see is slowly killing me,
Is killing you, is killing us, so's the number 37 bus
As it belches forth the fires that scorch
This dusty orb that we daub
With our pain, our polluted rain,
They say it's all in vain, maybe I'm just a little insane.
But aren't we all deep down inside? In that little place where we
                                                                           crawl to hide.
I don't know, I couldn't say, who am I anyway?
And still the words want to flow but one day I'll just have to let it go,
But not today, nor yesterday.
Maybe tomorrow I'll drown in sorrow
Or the empty glass that marks the time with the level of its wine.
And slowly we just slip and slide to that place deep down inside,
That the fire which bellows forth can no longer ever scorch.

Jonathan Wood

EVERLASTING PEACE

Twenty five years of heartache, destruction, tears and pain,
Wondering what it was all about, and what any of it would gain,

Families have lost their loved ones, whom no other can replace,
Although left with lots of memories, in their hearts lie an empty space.

Finally the talking started, to get the violence to cease,
So we could finally be on our way, to everlasting peace.

Everyone danced and sang in the streets, when the news did
finally come through,
There was now an end to the bombing, and the guns were silent too.

Our city came to life once more, new businesses came to town,
The soldiers were being sent back home, towers and checkpoints,
were taken down.

Then on Friday the 9th of February, after 17 months had passed,
Came the news that no-one wanted to hear,
That peace wasn't going to last.

Just one hour later, in a quiet London town,
A massive bomb exploded, pulling a business premises down.

100 people were injured, 2 more were found to be dead,
All our hopes of going forward, were now back in reverse instead.

I was only 9 when the troubles started,
Things were fine until then, I've been told,
My one wish, for myself and my family now,
Is that peace returns, before we grow old.

Frances Meenan

YOUR NIGHT, MY DAY

As I sleep my day begins;
What dreams I have, you will never know;
All bright and happy they are;
How I wish you were there.

Our laughs, those smiles, I can only sigh;
No need to walk or run as you all can do;
I just dream and watch my life go by;
Must they end, those days of wonder?

As always a gentle voice beckons me awake;
Yet as I say *no* each time;
It is no use, I have to stir;
Knowing that another night must come;
When I can close my eyes and let another day begin.

James Nimmo

MY FATHER WARNED ME

How can these steel-gates open so easily?
My Father once warned me to,
'Beware of the door that never creaks
Watch out for the well-greased hinges
The slightly open eye'

Did he say this with one hand raised in
anger and the other lowered in guilt,
or are these words just my own built-up
images and waxwork lies?

With all these thoughts racing through my
head, I silently press the bell that will
always ring.

Paul Yussarian

UNTIL THE NEXT TIME...

Life resumes some semblance
Of normality
Eventually
Until, from out the blue,
The missing hits
As a huge wave
Strikes a boat
And tosses me into
That turmoil of despair
Yet again
Crashing at my heart,
Crushing it,
And I'm adrift once more.
It will subside
I know now that it will
And once again I'll feel
Some sense of equilibrium
... Until the next time.

Jill Myers

TAKE SUMMER

Only the sound of the sea
All is forgotten,
No child crying
No seagull flying
Faded beach huts abandoned
Grimly shuttered, locked or broken.
Unturned pebbles washed and waiting
Their capture, now that summer's gone.

Peggy Parfitt-Moule

THOUGHTS

The mind dwells on the wrong thought,
and anger and hatred fill the mind,
suddenly one has been caught,
peace and tranquility are left behind.

One looks in the past,
and remembers how bad people have been,
already the shadows are cast,
in darkness life cannot be seen.

If one looks at life through hate,
it seems so dirty and low,
yet good thoughts so easily create,
a happiness that others know.

How easily prejudice changes one,
from good to emotional extremes,
balance and logic becomes inhuman,
and hate and anger fill one's dreams.

Such purity lies within,
a purity of body and mind,
one must stay away from sin,
and bad thoughts that evil will find.

Saleh Chaudhri

SURVIVAL

Imprisoned by poverty on the streets
Exhausted with hunger in an affluent town
Chilled by the coldness of a community
Despondent with loneliness amidst the masses.
An open wound that never heals.

Jean Drummond

ISLE OF YOU

Where warm winds blow
And sunrise breaks
Amid the halcyon sea,
There lies an isle
Of beauty bound
Where love can wander free.

With swaying palms
And golden sands
That storms have never seen,
With sun-kissed flowers
Of rainbows shade
And wondrous fields of green.

Where words are heard
Upon the breeze
So soft and sweet and true,
And here I'll stay
With your consent
Upon the Isle of you.

Pray, rest your hand
Upon my chest
And know this heart is yours
For you and I
Are all alone
Upon these golden shores.

I'll hold you close
And whisper words
So soft and sweet and true
And you may hold
My heart, my soul
And know that I love you.

Scott H Mitchell

SUMMER TO FALL

Summer's colourful confidence,
Painted all over my face:
And your arms,
Squeezed me tight with security,
And your body,
Smothered my soul with its intimacy,
My truth, a paradox of fallacy,
How my hope was displaced.

What a whirligig image!
Spinning my head with delusion:
And your lies,
Tempted the likes of my innocence,
And your games,
Coaxed my words of defence,
My trust, a fading commodity,
Ever pervading confusion.

Samantha Allen

WARNING

Children run like soldiers,
around about the mist,
disused and abandoned
stray and functionless,
their spirits scream
like falcons,
their eyes they gleam
like beacons,
a signal to the unjust
and a welcome to the
heavens.

Sally Brighten

MY LIFE

The simple things of life, mean most of all to me
Lovely little leafy lanes, the splendour of a tree
By the rippling winding streams I spend many happy hours
Shapes and colours all unique in the beauty of the flowers
Quietness and stillness in nature all around
Birds upon the treetops make a lovely sound
Keep very still and I may see rabbits playing in the grass
They bob down a burrow fast if people start to pass
The contrast to my other world is when I get back home
Children noisily chattering, never ever leave me alone
I love their energy and life and seeing them having fun
Running jumping climbing, sticky hands in butter
Toys and books upon the floor oh what a lot of mess
and clutter!
Cooking cleaning washing clothes, trying to be a good wife
With my husband and my children, I would never change my life.

Mabel Josephine Harrison

ME TROUSERS

Trying my hand in pockets of time
To find them half-full, full of bits
or fraught lined
Tightening my belt, but saving my cash
Only amounts to lost time that I've stashed

Split seams
Flappin' in the wind
That's how my days seem to end and begin

But if being ironed out
Means being pressed flat and plain
I'll keep rolling down mountains
And jumping off trains!

S J McCluskie

LIFE'S BUMPY ROAD

The roads are bumpy, they're not flat,
Life's a little bit like that.
When everything looks smooth and clear,
Around the corner trouble's near.
When everything in the street,
Looks so tidy and so neat,
You don't see that little crack,
You trip and fall and hurt your back.
The road ahead looks quite all right,
Down comes the fog to give you a fright.
If you take a wrong turn and don't go back,
You'll find it a long and lonely track.
Look at life this way and you may despair,
But don't, lots of people really do care.
If your car breakes down and will not go,
Along comes someone to give you a tow.
When things look bleak and rather grey,
Someone will come to show the way.
When you travel life's winding lane,
Sometimes there's joy sometimes there's pain.

James Stuart Denby

AN ISOLATED MOMENT

When waiting in silence
Extended minutes sound like hours
The stillness smothers in harmony
And is then startled
By one solitary intrusion
Of noise.

Lesley Jane Grimes

THE EFFECT

Smothering orange lights the night sky
A flash and crack of lightning reaches my eye
To view such an electrifying event
The thrills, the chills and adrenaline rush sent

Dark possessed clouds assemble up above
Is this Mother Nature's showing of love
As the rain searches down, to dampen our thoughts
Terrorising people of all kinds and all sorts

To see the soul stripping spectacle
To hear the roar, and the killer tentacles
Rain, rain suppresses summer's happiness
To me it is an honour just to be a witness

The heart stopping sound, heard by all miles around
Shaking and breaking the sodden ground
Children hiding under their comforting beds
Me with thoughts racing through my head

It's a great chance, to put pen to paper
For uncontrollable restless sleep later
The thrill, the chill will remain for days
As I stare out my window, a slave but to gaze

Through every bone, I feel the groan
Through every vein, I feel excite - the light
To realise the drive
To exist, to be alive
The effect.

Caroline Mitchell

THE NAVIGATOR'S LANTERN

Appearing near, and yet so far
do not hasten o' guiding star.
Your presence in the sky at night
shining there, a welcome sight.

Shoot not shoot as some stars do
but stay forever we would choose.
Yours, a heavenly shroud of mystery
while ours alas is history.

Sailors, shepherds and wise men too
watch your progress, all in tune.
By sea or land they are bound
there arriving, safe and sound.

Douglas Boswell

GOSSIP MONGERS

To bend and twist the truth about
A favourite pastime right enough.
So easy for some folks to do
Without a thought for consequence.
Is it to punish for some
Unacknowledged guilt.
To make all mankind the same.
To bear the brunt, to pay where
Payment should be none.
Shall innocence thus be destroyed
In some macabre game.
To lower the status
To those perpetrators
And make all equal.

E Dibb

SHADOWS

See no evil,
Hear no evil,
Convictions of a once honest mind
      encircled in doubt.
Conspiracies, calculated and ruthlessly cold,
Unyielding deceptions accumulate.
      Where do we go *now?*

Cynical homelands, Earth
turning about your denatured axis
Throwing long shadows when sun is high
bleeding my eyes as His wept in Golgotha,
How came you to be?
Science, cynic, lover or myth?
Man is one of too many,
Almighty primate knows so little of so much
      and gives less in return.

The obvious no longer exists.

      See
'no evil'
      Hear
'no evil'

As shadows claustrophobically encircle the pitiful remembrance
      of what, once,
        could
      Have been.

Shân Ellis

UNTITLED

Why do I sit and gaze at the skies?
Why do I sigh with the wind?
Why do I cry when the rain falls down?
I know no answer to this

All that I know when I see all these things
That my heart cries out to you
Just wanting to know that you love me still
In the way that you used to do

In the winter I watch as the snow floats down
All the way from the heavens above
But all of the time I am dreaming of you
And longing to share your love

A Rowlands

REBECCA

When I first saw Rebecca
My tears I tried to hide
This was my first grandchild
My heart was filled with pride
The memories of that beautiful day
No-one can ever take away
You're the first born
From my little boy
And always will be
Grandma's pride and joy
With big blue eyes and smiling face
Your photographs take pride of place
From mammy, dad, grandparents too
You'll have lots of love
And we'll give thanks every day
To the Lord above
For giving us a beautiful treasure
And one that gives us so much pleasure.
If there comes a time in your life
When you need to shed a tear
I hope you remember Rebecca
Grandma's always here.

J Robinson

UNTITLED

Sometimes I'm so lonely,
sometimes I'm so sad,
sometimes life just gets me down
then I feel so bad.
My temper rises, my patience slips away,
I go to bed and cry for hours
till night turns into day.
There seems to be no end at all
to all my worries now,
the laughter and the smiling face
disguise the fact somehow
that deep inside I'm hurting
like I've never hurt before,
I'm trapped inside by guilt and failure
of that you can be sure.
My children are so strong and good
I dare not let them see -
that what their mother really is -
a failure that is me.
I want to give them so much more,
I can't now - that I know,
I've had my chance,
I've blown it and I've let them down for sure.
But what I did, I did for them,
even though it all went wrong,
please forgive me children for I've loved you all along.

Brenda Schubert

ALL ALONE

All alone in a room . . . so quiet and still
If I open my mind . . . the air it would fill
So many thoughts . . . there to see
So many dreams . . . there to be.

All alone with ideas . . . in my head
Feeling so much . . . to what was said
Emotions flying . . . to and fro
Emotions there . . . ready to show.

All alone in this world . . . is your mind
Working within . . . all mankind
Searching for . . . a way to you
Searching for . . . that dream too.

Gayle L Norcross

SCHOOL DAYS

School days are the happiest,
Days of your whole life,
I bet whoever said this,
Eats their peas with a knife!

In other words, they must be mad,
This saying just can't be true,
Can you remember having fun?
That's what I'm asking you.

And yet when I really think back,
To those long forgotten days,
We did have lots of good times,
In so many different ways.

There were school trips to the seaside,
Choir practice and school plays,
Nature walks in summer time,
On lovely golden days,

So when you're sitting at your desk,
Whiling the hours away,
Remember, these days are your happiest ones,
It really is true what they say.

A C Churcher

BYGONE DAYS OF OLD

Four-thirty now and time to rise
Now slumber's played its part,
The sleepy heads to waken
New days about to start.

A cold November morning
The cobbled streets are damp,
The dairy cart horse, patiently
Waits by a loading ramp.

The urchin who's been sleeping rough
The weary look, those eyes,
He scavenges the market bins
To find food, how he tries.

An eerie look about the streets
As mantles brightly glow,
The postman whistles, sparks his clogs
Six street, then home he'll go.

One by one, the houses show
That people are awake,
But not the first, aroma tells
That bread is on the bake.

Minutes pass, the town begins
To come to life and so,
The shoppers choose their wares, trudge home
Oh no! Here comes the snow.

The kids in shoes that have no soles
Throw snowballs, smile with glee,
A snowman slowly rises. Oh look!
Another's here, look there, that's three.

In time the day drifts gently by
The men return home, cold,
They prayed for brighter 'morrows
In those, bygone days of old.

Charles Smethurst

OUR DREAM

May I lie in your arms
    all night
While our bodies are spent
    and the shadows have gone
Shall we dream
    the same dream
With you everything is right
    and nothing is wrong

Floating aimlessly
    above the night
We can play hide and seek
    with the stars
Sit and talk with
    Mr Moon
Looking down at our sleeping bodies
    from afar

Hearing the beating of
    a distant drum
I remember, it is not a drum
    but your heart
You move and hold me
    even closer
Our lives are entwined together
    never to part.

Louise Ann Jolliffe

THE TREE

He stands there in my line of vision
Each day as I tend my work
So tall and proud and elegant
Despite the elements he cannot shirk.
His pride seems hurt in winter
As mother nature strips him bare
But come the spring that pride is restored
As new life emerges and drinks in the air
How long has he stood there, the world at his feet?
How much has he seen, things he'll never repeat?
He'll go on standing there long after I've gone
He'll witness much more and grow ever strong
How I wish I could share in his strength and long life
To be part of the changes, new problems, new life
But as a mere mortal my wish cannot be
And I'll continue to envy my strong, handsome tree.

Julia Boyle

CHILD

The child in between is a very sad child.
She loves both and wishes for a kiss and a smile
But when things go wrong she sits in the dark
and remembers the times as she played in the park
Torn in between which way to go. What will
happen nobody knows
Trying to remember things that were good
Turn back the clock
If only she could.
The love for them both never will die
But a time to remember is only to cry.

M Bartley

MOONLIGHT

No blinding light from sovereign cup
Nor wealth, nor city magnate share
Could half suppose to have the right
To stand with gentle moonlight.

Believers, as believers do
Confess to her their secret loves
To wish, content to know she will
Betray no confidence.

The silvered statue knows her grace
Madonna of the golden Broom
In silent midnight meetings passed
Their unfamiliar truth.

Dew glistened threads in nimble weave
Contend her eerie morning gown
In convolution lacing fold
The spinner's toil is done.

Virtue betrothed to secret night
Relinquished at the kiss of dawn
Long banished with his golden orb
To linger dispossessed.

His mighty crock of battle gold
Sustaining day in noble span
Till falling dusk knows of the night
her softness dwells within.

Pale peace usurping crimson crown
To hide, but subtle, his survey
In tantalising moonlight shafts
That disregard the day.

C J Toyne

FEAR

'Twas in the darkness creeping
Through minds he'd met before
Thoughts he'd scoured with venom
Dripping power from every pore.

In silence they cannot stop him
His passion too great, too strong
For all who lie in innocence
Are victims before too long.

Night time carries him swiftly
From the depths no man can see
And when silence so engulfs them
He slips inside their dreams.

He strips their souls so naked
Bearing spirits who cannot cope
As he devours each drop of life
From eyes who see no hope.

The only armour within yourself
To guard you when he's here
Is do not sleep or dream tonight
For in your mind he's near.

He'll catch you at your weakest
But hide when you are strong
Freezing time around your body
You'll be his until the dawn.

Lynne Browne

THE CHASE

Here it is, she says
I'm holding it with both hands
And when I let it go
I free your heart's desire

With gentle persuasion
Her hands give way
   To release a beautiful butterfly
        Such golden wings
           So delicate
               And gentle
                    It flies up into the air
                          And far away

There it goes, she says
It's all your dreams come true
And all you have to do
Is catch it.

Chris Lee

ECHO MOUNTAIN

I climbed a mountain
Walked on the air
Everything silent
No-one was there -
Out of that silence
I suddenly heard
A whisper of wind -
The song of a bird.
White clouds above me
Not very high
I felt if I tried I could just
touch the sky.

Barbara Dennerly

ADDICTION

A glimpse of you, amidst the gloom
Draws brightness to the darkest room
I see you and cannot resist
A touch of you, a gentle kiss

They tell me that I must abstain
My love for you will be in vain
A dark desire may be pursued
But pain and sadness will ensue

You represent the purest sin
One scent of you and I'm reeled in
Power of will can ne'er defy
The craving that you satisfy

Alas, I know we can't go on
My love for you is, sadly, wrong
I realise I must let you go
The truth is out for all to know

You are my comfort, that is fact
When I'm with you, I'm so relaxed
But I'll survive, that will be seen
Without you, demon nicotine.

M Wojtaszek

MY GRANDSON

One day while I was out at work, I got a call to say
You've got a baby grandson, born at 10 o'clock today
I couldn't wait to see him this little baby boy
Who made a difference to my world, and filled my heart with joy

His little face was chubby, his hair as black as jet
And even though he's ten years old, I can see that baby yet
Right now he's quite a smart young man, for fashion is his aim
He never would wear anything, that hasn't got a name

He knows designer fashion, Oh! He's really very cool
He's quite a pleasant fellow, and so popular at school
I enjoy every Monday, when he comes to us for tea
When he grows up no girl on earth, can love him more than me

I have one special picture, imprinted on my mind
Of a young lad with a cheeky grin, and mud on his behind
And in the distant future, when he grows to six foot three
I hope he'll still have time to come, and have his Monday tea.

Eileen Whiston

SUNRISE OVER CASTLETOWN HARBOUR

The sun awoke over the harbour
Light fell on the still sleeping town
Seagulls, surf and beating hearts,
Were the only sound.

As the sun rose over the harbour,
And the moon, its light grew less.
Awaiting one word of the sun, to say go,
With the past to your rest.

For the future is with the sun,
And ours had just begun,
Like the radiant light of the dawn
Our symbol of love was born.

As the sun ascended the harbour
The day unfolded its new;
Design, a golden sun embossed
On a ceiling of blue . . .

When the sun awoke over the harbour
And I fell in love with you.

Julie Ann Sloan

A BRIGHT OCTOBER DAY

Full of sadness not shock,
When first we received the news.
It was only confirmation, of what already we believed.

My colleagues at tea breaks if the subject was ever raised,
Knew exactly who was at risk,
and who was most to blame.
It's gays, lesbians, and junkies,
No-one that would be missed.

Against such narrow mindedness,
it's hard to make any ground.
More so if it stops their enjoyment when
'the boys go out on the town'.

Filled with sadness, sorrow, and disquiet,
That such parting brings.
My colleagues offer condolences,
Though not a word is taken in.

They thought it must be cancer,
How could they suspect,
Even with your passing there's no mention of it yet.
Not once during the funeral,
Though the minister had enough to say.
As he thanked those around us,
For the love and care they gave.

We each sat without moving, our reddened eyes filled with tears,
No comfort could I give,
To those I held most dear.

Though friends are gathered round you.
Their laughter is far away,
For company only mourners, on this bright October day.

James Gold

UNTITLED

In hope's rosy haze
Through which I live my days and ways
Do I ever stop and think what will come after?
And when I think about it all, do I come across a wall
That's made of tears and lives inside the laughter?
Shall I wake one day and find, that *sans-facade* has struck me blind,
And in doing so has opened up to me,
The way things really are, the clinging to a pointless star,
And the fear of one day knowing how to see?
And for a moment standing there, at the bottom of the stair,
I'll find the time to climb and then to die.
And when I've torn the landscape from the page, and screwed it all up in a
                                                                 moment's rage,
Will I then realise with fear what I have lost?
Will I turn and walk away, to where once there was a day,
And tearfully begin to count the cost.
And when time begins to stall, I'll stand naked in the hall,
And turn from open door to open door.
And then I'll step into the light, that hides inside the darkest night
And never think of what I was before.
Or will I simply be the same
Sad fool within the foolish game,
Feeling for the corners of the board?
Never squeeze my heart and mind into my hand and then decide
To tie them up with death's soft silver chord.
For between the minutes of each waking hour,
When all that lies within begins to cower,
There hides there what the mesh of life denies.
And when death pulls back the drape,
And tears what *I* am out of shape,
The shapeless thing looks up towards the skies.

Mark Anderson

OF WEATHER AND SANITY

Wind, rain and blue skies meet my gaze
I reflect upon my innocent daze
Am I one or are we all
together lost, as one I fall

Inside of self, within another
rolling over fires to smother
freely letters etch the feeling
lazy innermost is reeling

Rock and roll and reel and feel
realities less driven wheel
of fortunes modest and sublime
I kick against lest they be mine

So to sense and nonsense all
inside is stretched up tall to fall
If fall I must, if must I shall
be surely broken, raving man.

M B Tildesley

DREAMLAND

With heads on our pillows, snug deep in bed,
Mother's kiss swept over each brow as she said,
Close your sleepy eyes now, the sandman's on his way,
Bedroom door softly closing, her footsteps crept away.

Suddenly a tapping, heard on the window pane,
We saw a little figure beckoning, calling,
Come join our game.
Looking through the window, full moon shining bright,
Stars twinkling, clouds floating fluffy white.

Running into the garden bathed in early dew, behold,
We saw fairies, gossamer wings, dresses of delicate hues.
The elves and the pixies in velvet, of brown, green and blues.
We danced and sang, played hide and seek,
Peeked into flowers to see bugs, bees furled in sleep.

Then a noise so crystal clear, of footsteps down the hall,
Grabbing hold of moonbeams we landed back into bed.
With sleepy eyes, and tousled hair, we heard our mother call,
'Come on children, up you get, leave your dreams behind.'
But with secret smiles, as we got dressed,
We knew, it was no dream at all.

P Simpson

A GOOD LIFE

The one thing to always remember
Is no-one is better than you
And lying's the biggest reminder
To only yourself you're untrue

Forget what is past and look forward
To good days your life has in store
By bad days you soon won't be bothered
But maybe you'll still look for more.

Life is all that you make it
And all that you want it to be
Never think you cannot make it
Live just how you want life to be.

I know we can't alter the bad times
But we can make life easy to bear
And also make good times much better
Simply by just being there!

Janise Murrie

WILD THING

Untamed - free
Born free of Free Spirit
Not shackled by convention
Free to move in any direction

Any shape. Any size
True to form
Honest throughout
No lies nor deceit
Childlike
Virgin
Pastures green

No stopping and starting
Living and dying
In life there is death
And in death there is life
A Phoenix born anew

From the depths of despair
To the heights of elation
Wave upon wave
Never ending
On an eternal journey
Forward side together
Form a circle
Then a square
An eternal triangle
In Saint Vitus' Dance
Before rigor mortis sets in.

Bill Craggs

THE COME-BACK CAT

I am the come-back cat
Gut strung, out-stretched
Hand slapped and pulled back
Turned, stomach churned.

I am the queen of hearts'
Break-away child
Hood over head over heels
Dug in my dug out.

I am the non-changing smile
And the world laughs
A minute being
Human, ever-erring

I am the kicked-while-down
Deep-hearted; too feeling, reeling
Thrown-back fish -
Netted octopus who ate his arms.

I am the spinning-top
Spun and forgotten
Faces all ephemeral as I am falling
Star that failed to shine.

I am the yo-yo's yo
String placed pleadingly in palms
Begging alms, wrapped around fingers
Pulled up and pushed down.

Though I am the constant friend
Ships sink when I blink
Back again lighthouse dreams
Shattered on human rocks.
What a sham.

Johanna S Emeney

TIME AND THE TIDE

The tide comes in
Salty fingers stroke the sand
Reaching out
Stretching for the land
Their caress is soft
But with the rising of the wind
Their fists pound the shore
Punish rocks as though they've sinned
The ocean spray
I taste the salt upon my lips
The wind is raw
Around my hooded face it rips.
The wind abates
The sea's anger dies away
Debris on shore
The guts torn out of the bay
The tide goes out
The beach will bare its soul
Footprints washed away
I was never here at all.

Helen Wheeler

DESIRE

Many things do we desire,
Some of which may fill us with greed,
Others we are lucky to acquire,
The remainder we still need.
When there is no love, there is fear,
Fear of insignificance, fear of loss,
Will we not shed a tear?
For those with obstacles to cross?

There is desire and hatred,
In a human confused by life,
It fails to sleep in its bed,
When its mind is wielding a knife.
It is conscious of its weakness,
Yet knows it is intelligent,
Can we help solve its bleakness?
And banish thoughts of resentment?

Humanity is not perfect,
Constantly learning the truth,
It has suffered too much neglect,
Too many dangers for the youth.
Some have learnt the art of restraint,
Human nature can be savage,
Can we live without complaint?
Do we really think we can manage?

J D Hart

HEALTHY LIFE

Throughout the medical world today,
Intelligent, professionals will not hesitate,
To give us all a pleasant, and healthy fate.
Pollutions, including nicotine that excruciate,
Those antisocials will continue to aggravate.
All those pollutions we find, leave
Incapacitated, those whom, or whatever, needs to breathe.
Advertisements, heavy fines, may attribute,
Those poisonous fumes, afflictions to be eliminated.
While attention is drawn, to all of our fate,
There are those, who will stay mentally blind,
To the health of the human race,
Will still blow their nicotine smoke, in our face . . .

B Marshall

HARDLY HELP

I could hardly help hearing
The warm wind
Making its way north
In the evening.

Yes. The light
Was worth watching:
Its spell of symbolism
Was hope passing.

Clouds trailed their shadows
Over the green valley
As lanes of birds twittered
From their hawthorn worlds.

To tell the truth:
You missed nothing.
Blood trickles on.
No thunderfall

Cascades the heart.
No bright emotion here
To light the way
Or lift us up.

Nothing is what it was
Worth recording.

John Harkin

FINAL PASSION

As within the embers of a dying fire,
A sudden spurt of spark attempting to rekindle
The now fast failing funeral pyre,
Which to ashes soon will dwindle.

My life now in its waning years
I liken to such fireside scene.
From warmth to coldness now it nears,
Though all but dead this spark e'er gleams.

Maybe what's left of life is thus,
Perhaps still the thrill of coming contest.
Who knows - before the body's dust -
One last romantic final conquest

C R Spillett

MY GRANDAD

My grandad sat in his rocking chair
                A lonely soul, but proud.
Not wanting pity or fussing about -
Not even talking aloud.
Thinking of things from bygone days
Memories of deeds said and done,
Wondering, what happened to - old you know who
And what became of his son?

Through the door came a little girl
She was the apple of his eye,
'Grandad,' she said, 'will you fix this for me?'
'Give it to me,' he said , 'I will try.'
She handed him her precious doll
Knowing he'd do the rest,
For he loved her, and would do anything
To prove he loved her best.

Age and youth, heads bent together
In perfect harmony
They really understood each other
That's how it will always be.

J E Madlin

LIFE

Life is like a journey to somewhere far away
Somewhere that we've never been and do not know the way.
We pack our bags and choose our route, and set out bright and keen,
And spend the years searching for that place we've never seen.
Sometimes the journey's calm and clear, we see our way for miles.
But sometimes clouds and storms appear and wash away our smiles.
For a while we lose our way and going on is a strain,
But the sun will always reappear, and on we go again.

Sometimes the road is long and smooth, we carry on without a care,
But then we change direction, and the load becomes too hard to bear.
The road turns dark and rough, and jagged rocks obstruct our way.
But on we go through perils and hurt until we see the light of day.

When we come to crossroads we don't know which way to turn,
Through our mistakes we get it right, by experience we learn.
There are no signposts on this journey to show which way to go,
No maps or compasses to help, by instinct we just know.
There is no way of seeing what is round every bend,
But just by trusting judgement we will get there in the end.

There are times through life when we can sail, or fly up in the air,
Then we always come back down to earth and carry on from there.
So don't despair when things go wrong and you seem to loose your way,
For although we all take different paths, we all meet up some day.

J Baybutt

IN LOVE

Waiting in anticipation,
Waiting for the phone to ring,
Distant music plays a quiet love song,
When he arrives I hear angels sing,
He says there's no love only lust,
Through these eyes he's a king.

There's more than just a physical attraction,
More than he'd like to admit,
Sometimes I feel I'm going to burst,
The passion burns like flames in a fire,
When we're together it's like a candle that's lit,
The flames are growing higher and higher.

Like an owl just seen at dusk,
When dawn breaks he's gone with the moon,
Maybe all this is pure lust,
But I know he'll be back
Very soon.

R M Hancock

RAINBOWS

Rays of the sun shining through droplets of rain
Performing a recital of the spectrum across a dampened sky.
An arc of colours which for a short while does remain
Until the air above us is once again warm and dry.

Rainbows are beautiful, they are a source of wonder.
Some people even dream of the gold that is said
To have been left by the fairies at one end o'er yonder
Our imaginations by such legends are gently fed.

The colours of the spectrum which make this glorious arc
Are placed in curves, a glorious medley of hues.
There's green, yellow, orange and red each making their mark
Topped by indigo and violet, majestic shades of the blues.

The colours all mingle together in the sky
They assemble to make a joyous creation
Of beauty - making us wish we could fly
And touch the rainbow in complete adoration.

Ros Silom

AS I WALKED ON THROUGH THE STORMY WATERS

As I walked on through the stormy waters,
I heard the angels cry.
It floated down to greet me,
and echoed through the sky.
Its cry was sweet and tender
and I knew I had no choice,
I had to follow the voice
The path was hard and lonely
and full of hate and war.
But all the while it was worth it,
For I knew I had the best,
The best this world could give.
The path of life may be hard and long
but that will surely pass.
And when it does you'll find
the key to happiness.

Elizabeth Hall

ALWAYS ALONE

Today was the day I found out the truth
I realised I'd reached the end of my youth
Stuck in a world that doesn't make any sense
My body, my mind, my soul so tense
Alone forever my life my own
All their hearts are made from stone
Trapped in a life of deceit and betray
Happiness gone and moved away
Split between two, torn apart
Eternal solitude, a broken heart
Misunderstood standing alone
Isolated always on my own.

Gemma Bodsworth

I ONCE HEARD THE WIND

I once took a peep, when the old wind blew
At the place where my flower stood all on its own,
I once heard a whispering, telling stories of you
And how tall that old flower had grown,

Let us walk right now, together, hand in hand
By the river of all rivers away,
And let us tell secrets of what is so grand
As time will not want to stay.

Never let go of the gifts that are here
Use them and show them around
'Cos one day, he'll come and it will be clear
You'll have to return, like a sound

Goodbye for now, I love you so much
We'll be together again, you will see,
Another flower has grown where the winds touch
And oh look it's right next to me.

I once took a peep when the old wind blew
At the place where my flower stood all on its own
I once heard a whispering telling stories of you
And how tall that old flower had grown.

Matthew John Leeming

LOST

Like a dream that fades in the light
Your image is lost as day into night

I, like a boat upon a shore
Shipwrecked by love that is no more

A black cloud in what was perfect sky
Marks my return to a solitary I.

Tanya Lloyd

WITH YOUR LOVE

With your love I'll be strong with your love to guide me all life long, by your side I can be anything you want me to be, with your love, to hold me all life long, with your love.

With your sweet love I'll not be lonely, with you beside me I can face all that life can bring, all I need is your love to hold me, with the love you give me all that your heart can bring. With all your kisses You can thrill me, be beside me till all the hurt passes away, with your love with your love.

With your love I'll be loving all the things you are for me just for me your love will hold me, I'll think of you and always be there beside you, I know you love me. Darling I get so weary days are long nights are the loneliest I've known, with your love I'll see the dawn, wake in your arms in the morning sun, dream the dreams with you to hold me, all life long all life long with your love with your love.

J M

ON MY MIND

I know I think of you far too often,
You rarely leave my mind.
Always there deep down inside,
Escape I cannot find.
I'm aware I'm leaving here far too soon
For things to happen between us, I know
That if you cared too you would have said,
Yet I wish that was not so.
Knowing these truths I'd like to erase you from my mind,
But that I can't do.
For I cannot choose what occupies my thoughts,
And right now, all I can think of is you.

Jane E Hughes

MIRANDA

She sails 'The Tempest' ship of fools
Amidst a fount of knowledge, we hear.
For then, alas, 'tis wisdom born of fact,
Not heartfelt fundamental feel
For words, life, language and forever.
She is calmed by Edmund
But he's no fool - a sage, a singer
Whose peace is within.
At home, a calm and solid rock
Works quietly there to ease her soul.
She draws.
She paints.
She reaches for 'The Pleasure Dome'.
She sings her mermaid songs
On calm and solid rocks, for real this time.
Hear her calling across the water,
Somewhere out there lies her cause.
Waves lap gently upon the stone
Whilst dolphins beckon her to distant shores.
She ponders.
She carries the awesome weight of decision.
She stands at the harbour's edge
And stares to find the horizon of her mind,
Where she can meet the sun and feel
Warmth on her skin.
To be herself and gain courage to change the world!
For now, she will sail 'The Tempest' ship of fools
But later storm the waves that hold her fast.

Linda Swain

SENIOR CITIZEN - 1996

How can it be - when old age was revered.
Through thousands of years - The Elders endeared.
What's wrong with this time - Senility a crime?
These people who fought - The 'War' - ghostly mime.
The lady is eighty - So her pension increased.
With 25 pence - She can have a great feast.
The money they've saved - for their final 'release'.
Is used in 'Means-Test' and aggravates peace.
So they hide their few pounds - in a place that seems safe.
And the 'thugs' - high on ecstasy - life-savings they 'rave'.
There once was a time in countries - worldwide.
When the senior warrior - was 'chief' of the tribe.
Then the young and the old - His wisdom would seek.
And decisions were made - to include mild and meek.
Society was strong - They contained all the throng.
They collectively hunted - with days full of song.
How can it be? when man is supreme.
That animals live better - or so it must seem.
They all know their places - within the same pack.
And some are more caring - 'Homo Sapien' do lack.
But that 'roofer' from Grantham - her head hung in shame.
And the 'blue-rinse' brigade - followed her - all the same.
aTo create a society - entrepreneur - to make rich.
And the 'old' and the 'wise' - 'Hooray Henrys' will ditch.
If you're poor and you're old - then you're out of the fold.
Then the young and the sick - their pockets we'll pick.

E A Healy

TRUE HORIZON

Where is truth's pledge in these storm-tortured skies?
        Subtleties swarm over the page; ink belies
            Whiteness beneath. Each shade upon shade
Of thought and fear clouds the purity which
Breathed the realisation. That I was you.

For a fleeting moment the horizon
        Shone white intensity, then blackened veils
        Struck out the sun. But stay your hand awhile;
Let only the presaging clouds ahead
Be captured in shadowy depths of ink.

Dona Packman

VIGIL

Will you come back again sweetest one, dearest one,
    Will you come back again love of my heart,
Say not goodbye, nor farewell oh my dearest one
    Let not death be the victor that tears us apart.

Use the strength of my body to hold back the darkness
    That entreats to enfold you within its cold shroud.
Use the surge of my lifeblood to fend off the reaper
    Banish him to the shadows, shout triumph aloud.

But already you're crossing that yawning black chasm
    To rest place of spirit where I cannot yet go
And I silently scream my hate and my anger
    To a God who is taking the one love that I know.

But I know in my heart it is selfishness only
    That seeks to detain you as you near journey's end
And this rending of soul is only a prelude
    To eternal reunion where broken hearts mend.

You'll not come this way again dearest one, sweetest one,
    You'll not travel this way again, love of my heart.
We'll not say goodbye but just an auf weidersehn
    Death can never be victor nor keep us apart.

Helen Bales

DOLPHINS

I watch the dolphins as they leap and play
Carefree, as if on holiday.
Droplets of water on shiny wet skin,
Who knows what dolphins think within.

As dolphins race through ripples galore
I come to like them even more.
Blue-grey bodies flow through the sea,
Coming closer, as tame as can be.

Ever moving, ever racing,
Dolphins ever, ever swimming,
Always happy, never crying,
They are always, always smiling.

Then away they go, into the sea,
Away as far as the eye can see.
      Away from me,
        The dolphins flee.

Eleanor Harris (10)

LIVING IN THE SILENT WORLD

I see birds fly, I hear no song
I see lightning, yet no thunder is heard
I live in a silent world
Hands sign what lips would say
Never have I heard the sound of happy children play
But I see their faces, it makes me smile
For seeing is believing
Hearing can be fooled
I live in the silent world
But I can see, touch, taste and smell
I know where and what I am
I see and believe, but the silence is deafening.

Amanda Rae Blair

A DAUGHTER'S LOVE

I walk up the stairs and hope to see
Her smiling face look up at me.
I open the door and glance around
She's slouched in the chair, there isn't a sound.
I call out 'Mum, it's only me'
She turns and squints and strains to see.
On recognition she smiles and lifts
Her outstretched arms to receive her kiss.
I stroke her hair, so snowy white
And hold her hand, so frail and light.
We sit and chat, and laugh and cry
And talk of days that have passed us by.
These precious moments shared together
Will be all that's left to remember forever.
And now it's time for me to go.
I wander alone in the winter's snow.
I can give her my love, give her my kiss
I don't know how she's got like this.
So love your mother while she's fit and strong
And even more so, when you won't have her long.

Patricia Parker

NOVEMBER MORNING

Early morning,
Warm vermilion streaking the sky,
Through the fickle transparent clouds.
The wet smell of November in the garden.
Dank leaves glued in papier-mâché forms,
Around the deep grass,
Luscious, steeped and moistened.
Sharp biting breath,
Stillness as if frozen.
Passive. Quiescent.

Stephen L Cleary

SON

I stand at the door and watch you go, tears in my eyes, but yet I know
That like a bird you needed to be, making your own way, strong and free.
Yet there is joy within my heart,
Each time we're together and then apart.
For the moment I held you on my knee you took part of my soul and kept
                                                                              the key.

It's been a source of wonder to me, as I've watched you grow.
You've touched my life and I have been blessed. I felt that you should know
Each day has been a treasure, with moments I could never measure.
How do you count a blessing, given from heaven above?

I think of a storm on a dark winter's night, power and majesty, yet with
                                                                              the light
A promise of peace at the moment of dawning, new beginnings in the
                                                                      silence of morning.
Trees turning gold with the rays of the sun, flowers gaining stature and
                                                                  beauty, each one.
Rain on your face, washing cares all away; the trust of a child, wanting to
                                                                            play.
All these and more are treasures to share, but none can measure or even
                                                                           compare
With the swell of my heart and the joy unfurled, thinking of you, being part
                                                                      of your world.

When you were small and I was tall
I cared for you each day.
Shared joy and laughter, wiped your tears
And set you on your way.

Now you are tall and I am small
I look up to see my son
With a mother's love and heartfelt pride
At the man you have become.

Annette Walker

I NEED A HUG
(Dedicated to my mother Lily Sherlow, deceased)

Allegedly nearer God in a garden
Surveying His wondrous hue
But dear departed mum
Here's where I feel closer to you.

Sitting among the nosing wasps and the
Butterflies and humming bees
Wishing you were here too
Sure I would pray this on my knees.

For I know how you loved the lilac, snowdrops,
And the violet with their blue
The lilac tree I promised mum
Is here now planted just for you.

Never a garden of your own in life and now
Since you have left me behind
Such as it is, my garden,
I've created with you in mind.

I visualise you often by this archway
Recalling eyes smiling through
I could grow melancholy
Our great chat's long overdue.

It's 'song at twilight' at this moment here mum
As I tour with water jug
Here's a rose for you
Oh mum I so need a hug.

Barbara Sherlow

THE WINDOW VIEW

God light, through white window pane,
Awakens me from the valley of dreams,
A shepherd sun with flock clouds,
Pop star flowers and pollen crowds.

Sunlight, like a first unknown love,
Warms my sleeping heart, and
The stretching suburban cold,
With fingers of glowing gold.

Pencilled horizon like a Picasso sketch,
Delicate lines, fragile lines like torn paper,
A masterpiece framed,
A pure thought unaimed.

Blowing grass, green as her emerald eyes,
Trees, firm, brown like the earth in which they stand,
The sky as blue as the deepest sea,
Drown in joy therefore,
At the view before me.

Justin Buckley

GREEN PAINT

Burning wax
Spurts from my ears
Splattering the girl who builds a shed
And still my head itches.

A full scene,
Meditatively enclosed and stopped.
From the slopes of a moss covered plant pot landscape
Around the rim or down a hill
Near a beach, somewhere with wooden posts
- someone comes to see me.

Chris Roland

THE SHORT CUT

I heard an owl screeching,
in the dark of the night.
Its ghostly call chills my bones,
it gives me such a fright.

My heart it beats much faster,
when I hear this lonesome call.
Must be the loneliness of this wooded place,
its trees they look so tall.

The air is damp the winds so cold,
This moon looks white and a face so old.
Moonbeams with their icy tone,
make my body feel like stone.

These trees take on the weirdest shape,
the dark wood surrounds me with its blackest cape.
A fox it screams like a baby's cry,
the sound is so near it seems nearby.

As I shiver in the midnight air,
no-one with me with this fear to share.
I feel the blood course through my veins
and my coat is soaked from driving rains.

And as I took a short cut through the wood,
this journey seems further than it should.
But it's too late now to just turn back
and my feet are cold from this muddy track.

I'm glad to be back home again,
out of the wind and the driving rain.
Familiar sights are all around,
it's good to be back and on home ground.

D M T Moore

A CHILD'S LEGACY

Don't tell the children
that the world will never be theirs,
or that no-one will ever answer their prayers.
Teach them not of misery and pain,
nor show them how to endure shame.
Let them reach the highest height,
without making their lives an endless fight.
Give them the strength to be strong
and know the difference between right and wrong.
Let them not be easily led
or believe all that they hear said.
Show them how to love and care
and dare to confront fear and despair.
Don't paralyse their quest for life
or make their journey one of strife.
Most of all, give them enough pride
to carry with them stride by stride,
so that even in their darkest days,
the memory of love forever stays.
Let them know what they are worth
for one day
this will be their earth.

Jez Ellison

A FURRY TALE

When our cat Henry passed away
It was a very sorry day.
He'd been with us for many years
We all sat down and shed some tears.

Some weeks ago the night was clear
When on our doorstep did appear
A very handsome tabby cat
Rather large and rather fat.

Next morning when the door was opened
He just strolled in - no word was spoken.
He looked around and settled down
I put him in the 'lost and found'.

No-one's claimed him to this day
So now we hope he's here to stay.
No longer does he need to roam
He's found himself a loving home.

Barbara Welsby

BLACK ROSES

Such a picture - beautiful.
Rosy red cheeks and a flawless complexion.
Flowing chestnut locks fall about her face.
Crystal blue eyes pierce the heart of any man.

Ivory lace-trimmed silk draped over her slender frame,
studded with pearls.
Elegant slippers protect her delicate dancing feet.
Embroidered gloves to disguise her hands.

A transparent tear trickles slowly down one cheek.
A tear of sorrow and recognition of what will never be.
Her posy wilts - pink rose petals fall to the ground.
Lying on the forest floor they nourish the soil.

It was not to be - obviously.
Destiny and fate weave an unfortunate spell.
The future joins the past - she is left with the present.
Such a cruel time to live . . . or die.

Helpless her body lies.
An open field of black roses.
The sparkle has left her eyes - her own heart pierced.
Prince Charming joins her.

Emma Satchell (16)

CHRISTMAS DAY

Baritone chimes the grey dawn greeted,
Calling forth the faithful few,
Crusted snow the hamlet coated,
As the gentle but cold wind blew.

Good wishes were most commonly spoken,
As each household its curtains drew,
Parcels were opened and wishbones broken,
As each family its Christmas knew.

Eased by TV's predicted repetition,
Day turned to dark night,
Only distracting those with indigestion,
Unnoticed by those with gastric delight.

Now Jack Frost his part did play,
As elderly pipes were burst and broken,
And water over furniture and fire did spray,
Leaving her with household all sodden.

Most were too full of Christmas spirit,
Her cries for help to hear,
But for two brothers good,
To whom private Christmas was not dear.

And so these three through kindness and need,
Found what others had lost,
And that which few now achieve,
True Christ's Mass.

A R Thompson

END OF MARRIAGE

The time -
for talk and tears
has passed.
The could have been
and might have been
no longer
have the ring of possibility.
The heart -
responds -
no more.
The only course - now seems
to be - to act
or very deliberately
to withdraw -
Cocoon one's isolation
avidly
Resent intrusions,
invitations - to again take part
in the magic paradox
and yet -
The scope - is so immense
the shades and colours
depths and heights
of human possibility
It seems - churlish
just to cast it
thus -
aside.

Barbara S Maclean

HIGHLAND DREAM

I heard the clicked shush of tide over shingle,
I felt the night breeze through an open window,
Love for a northern land washed over me
In passionate waves,
Kindling the fires which burst into the bright
flame of our mutual high summer;
I saw the beauty of shadowy glens,
Where time itself hung on mystery shrouded peaks,
Where lochs shone with sparkling promise,
Of things that were and things to be,
Where streams gushed forth true romance
of past and present;
Where love pours into the music of the heart
And makes a glorious perfume of the senses,
Like brilliant flowers bursting into bloom,
Their purple glory touched with gold
Beneath a shining sun;
I see the dream which was real,
May the truth in a dream,
Be in truth - reality!

Victoria Helen Turner

BEACH HOUSE

I'm drifting down beyond the waves.
I cannot stop. I cannot be saved.
The image has a wonderful feel,
Complete peace, yet so unreal.

I feel the warmth against my skin,
I hear someone calling me in.
A distant tapping, an eerie feel,
Yet I'm mesmerised and follow heel.

I've sunken to tremendous depths,
Time has put me to the test.
Life has reached its second phase.
Quite beautiful as if entranced in a daze.

This is the place I've been trying to find.
I no longer feel so deaf and blind.
Life so far has been so contrived.
I now feel much more alive.

Jayne Edney

UNCEASING DECEASED UNSUNG

Lush rain on impenetrable marble
as dark as black uncertain of itself,
with fading rivers of white ink tracing your name, and more,
who you were, are. Were.

Silent sound of all but rain gently drumming.
A door of marble opens my mind to you
but closes us off for my earthly ever.
As elusive in life; I search for ether, for psyche,
to understand you, to grasp and be able to hold on to you,
but distance and others' wrought emotions carry you further away.

Cool and detached, no, please, passive and constant,
the marble book lies open and unwritten in stone,
save details as sparse as my teeming hopes are vibrant.

I bend to remove the growing weeds, and single thistle,
argent verdancy littering your tidy, tended space,
pulsing milk blood it has no right to,
and with tender care, tend with care, timidly self-conscious,
I wait for tears that cannot come, though wished.
A love, unreal, that cannot end, because it has never known.

Rebecca Thomson

INFATUATION

To think you were once my everything
All those years ago
We were both much younger
but tell me did you know
That every time I saw you I made
a mental note
Of what you wore, what you did
and to whom you spoke.

To look at you were nothing special
only special to me
long blonde hair, average height and
fashion clothes of the day
but those eyes . . .
would take me miles away.

I knew so many things about you
tell me had you no idea?
That I worshipped you from afar
yet wished I could be near
'infatuation' they called it
'a teenage crush' they said

Why when I saw you the other day
did my head go dizzy
and my knees go weak
no my feelings for you
I'll always keep.

Gillian Mesce

WITH REFERENCE TO A FEMALE GARDENER, WITH HIP TROUBLE

The importance of mowing,
the pedantically well trimmed velvet,
question your green fingers, are not turning blue,
for the assistance of netball tactics,
will not help the potting problem,
the assault of the secateur,
the marriage,
do you take this seed, to be your lawfully wedded earth,
a rose can be beautiful,
would be beautiful,
yet gardening gloves, and a jar of quick grow,
will not always ensure,
the perfect bloom,
botany can easily be replaced,
but hips cannot.

Alan Curtis

DEATH OF A SPARROW

Death came to my window this morning
I never invited him there
He came with a crash and a flutter
Of tiny wings through the air
I went at once to your rescue
There was nothing that I could do
For your poor little heart was beating its last
I could only stay with you
When peace came to you my little friend
And I knew that now you were free
I gently lifted and buried you there
Beneath my favourite tree
But thoughts of you stayed with me all day through
And I am sure a part of me went with you

Maude A Ryder

THE LAST GOODBYE

The room was cold, I looked around,
My heart that made the only sound,
My body weak, my feet so numb,
I walked across to see my mum.
The coffin door was open wide,
I found the strength to look inside.
The last time ever I would see,
My mum laid there so peacefully.
The silks she wore, they caught my tear,
My eyes they filled with lonely fear,
Her face so pale, a lifeless frame,
Her life was gone, who was to blame?
And many thoughts ran through my head,
As she lay inside her new-found bed.
A rose I gave and placed with love
So that she could take it up above.
My mumbled words came from my heart,
'I love you mum we'll never part'.
I knew that it was time to leave,
So one last look, my pain to grieve,
I told her that I loved her so,
And told her that I had to go.
I walked so slow, the door shut tight,
My mum forever out of sight.
No longer would I see or touch,
The one thing that I loved so much.
The word goodbye meant forever that day,
I turned with fear and walked away.

Cheryl Morley

THE WAYWARD SON

Mother sits beside the window,
The flutter of the autumn leaves.
She doesn't see their golden colours,
Deep inside my mother grieves.
Long ago she whispers slowly,
When he was just a child of three
Tommy would sit here and chatter,
Watch the world from on my knee.
Gently mother counts the buttons
On her lacy blouse of blue,
Softly sings a childish song,
The way her little boy would do.
Then back again the street attracts her,
Up and down no-one in view
Her eyes fill up with tears of sorrow,
Oh please come home she's missing you.
If you could see the way she loves you,
The hours spent just waiting here
Her memories mixed up inside her
Anticipating only fear.
To stay away so long is cruel,
Our father died, she feels alone
Though I am always here beside her,
She only prays her son comes home.
Five years now since you decided,
No more a child, a man must roam,
But don't you think the time is ready,
The wayward son should wander home.

Angela O'Neill

NO FUTURE

It hurts me to close my eyes.
Lying down, thinking about the past.
Could I change what happened.
Or was it meant to happen.
As a child things were tall.
Holding my parents' hands
I felt insecure.
Growing up I felt the pain.
Turning from a child into a man.
No matter where I go, or what I see.
Wondering what's around the corner.
Love and hate, violence and war.
Darkens people's minds.
War in the past, war in the future.
Which way do we look.
To the stars above we can't look.
They're covered with pollution.
I guess the pain that I felt
Will stay until my death.
How I wish time would come
And make me secure
If it meant turning from a man
Back to a child.

Richard Wolfendale

GIVE AN EAR

Are we good at listening
        To what others have to say?
Or do we turn a deafened ear
        Or move our heads away?

There are many saddened ones
        Bereft of all to care,
Many who have hit hard times
        And only feel despair.

It must indeed grow wearisome
        When no turning marks the road,
And an ear that's sympathetic
        May help to ease their load.

If only now and then we made
        A point of talking less,
And listened, not just with our ears,
        But with hearts that can caress.

Olive M Cork

FAIRY LAND

The morning mist reveals a world,
that fairies only know,
Like fluffy clouds up in the sky,
it takes a while to go.

And as it lingers o'er the land,
the fairies they do play,
Around the toadstool rings they dance,
until the break of day.

And as the dawn lifts up its head,
and daylight slowly grows,
Silver studded spiders' webs,
light up the dark hedgerows.

All neatly laid across the grass,
one sees a silken cloak,
But as the sun begins to rise,
it fades away like smoke.

This is the place where fairies play.
How is it that I know?
The wise old owl revealed to me,
this secret long ago.

E J Sherwood

TIRED OLD TOWN

The wind blows cold, shutters are down,
Late summer in the seaside town.
The holiday months just came and went
And the weather wasn't heaven sent.

Tears on the windows of old guest houses
Old ladies on the prom in windswept blouses
The rock and candyfloss lie unsold
Collars are up against the cold.

Where are the families? All abroad.
Miami, Majorca, whatever they can afford
Guaranteed sun and clear blue skies
But they still eat burgers and greasy French fries.

The arcades still jingle in the seaside town
What else to do? The water's not blue
And the family pubs with no families there
Are struggling to sell their watered down ware.

But wait, there's life, if you look close enough.
Single mum, two kids, times are tough
Doing her best to stop them getting bored
Miami? Majorca? The seaside town's all they can afford.

Peter Harris

A NEW LIFE

In a world of war
Where peace has no meaning
A world of darkness
In which dreams are shattered.
There is, on the horizon
A tiny glimmer of hope.
For amongst the fighting.
Amongst the darkness and shattered dreams
A child is born.

A child so beautiful.
So sweet and innocent.
Knowing nothing of the destruction
That surrounds her.

For just one moment,
The fighting stops.
The world is silent.
Shattered hopes and dreams are rebuilt
As the people of the world
Witness a miracle.
The birth of a new life.

Lynn Harvey

HER AND HIS DREAMS

In her eyes
I see soft sunlight
which warms my winter's day.
In her eyes
I see pure love
for loved ones passed away.
In her eyes
I see cold oceans
which drown me as I breathe.
In her eyes
I see such sorrows
for which I can but grieve.

In her eyes
I see my silhouette
which slow shall fade away,
yet though this shade may leave her
his heart shall always stay.

D Turner

TIME TRANSCENDS US

One day our world will end.
When the birds have sung their last song,
When the river no longer flows through the land
and the sun sets for the last time,
Our world will end.

We travel our last journey,
Searching for the answers to our destiny.
Our earth bleeds and our skies weep
as we search ourselves for answers
Before time transcends us.

So many questions inspired by our ignorance,
So many answers pondered by our consciousness,
But it is out of our hands.
Life has a certain mystery,
There is no logic.

We long for childhood days of innocence,
And our undeveloped intelligence.
But now with the pages of our mind complete
we breathe our last breath, try to make our peace with freedom.
Yesterday is over.
Our world will end.

Gillian Lindsay

TUNNEL OF LOVE

I look down the tunnel
And what do I see
You standing there
Calling for me

I walk further in
You get further away
I'm hoping to touch you
Again soon someday

Why did you leave me
When we were in love
You left me alone
For the peace up above

I'm trying to reach you
By doing the same
And then when I do it
I'll be with you again.

Kelly Souten

BIRDS

Quietly listen,
Hear them sing,
Imagine the look in their eyes,
Are they eating the bread
I have thrown?
The unknown.
Through unseeing eyes
I can only imagine
Their size, their colour,
Their stature.
The songs they sing
Are cheerful,
To listen is beautiful,
Although unseeing I'm not fearful,
So why when they land
Do the cats pounce?
The sound of a gun,
Why shoot?
They sound like one of
God's many creations
So *why* the confrontation?

Marie Sullivan (14)

MAKE THAT SPECIAL FRIEND

Could you ever imagine yourself alone?
Having nobody there to talk to
When you really long for a friend
To love, honour and take care of you.

It must be sad to think of oneself
With a lonely and sorrowful heart
Longing to talk to your neighbour
But don't know where or how to start.

A lonely heart may feel resentment
Wondering why it's in this state;
It needs you, and only you, to decide
to make friends before it's too late.

Reach out for that special person
Who's willing to lend an ear;
Tell them of how you have felt
regarding unhappiness, shyness and fear.

That special friend is sure to come along
To help you along with a shove;
Between you could become a bond
Made up of faith, truth, honesty and love.

When you find that friend,
Be sure never to let them go;
Keep them like a treasured possession -
They're the greatest treasure to know.

Trina S Brown

HURST CASTLE

My silvery isle
In the Solent rest
Its very being fills my breast
I know it's there - my bones must rest

The triple rocks that forge the sea
Strong the lighthouse that guideth me
Tides of life will drift - I pray
The silence of the sailing boat
Will lament my soul away

Doreen J Quilter

SUNDAY

I wake up to the sound of Sunday
a lull hangs over the street
like a pall of smoke,
the world's in carpet slippers.

I can taste it is Sunday
the hustle and bustle of
the week fading on my tongue,
I savour the tang of inertia.

The smell is ripe of Sunday,
the perfume of a different day
invades the air,
I inhale the scent of otherness.

I see it is Sunday, no letters,
there's no commuter rush and hurry.
Churches are wide open and hopeful,
shops looking coy for intruding.

Feel it is Sunday, I reach out
and touch the aura
surrounding a deviant day.
Massage the distinction until,
it slips away on Monday.

Mary Gilhooly

REMEMBRANCE

Once there was a tall green forest,
The scent of pine was in the air,
It teemed with life in all its forms
From a tiny ant to a powerful bear.

And even taller than the forest
Stood the mountains capped with snow
Where the eagle flew from its rocky nest
And only the bravest men would go.

And the sunsets used to be like magic
Like a fire burning in the sky,
Till the night had settled like a blanket,
With the mellow light of the moon on high.

The most amazing thing though to my mind,
Was how we were so terribly blind,
We didn't stare with a childlike gaze
At the constant miracles that filled our days,
But convincing ourselves of our own evolution
We continued to spew our mindless pollution.

And now we dream of our paradise lost
And realise to our great cost,
That never again will the tall pine stand
On our poisoned acid rain-soaked land.

Darryl Williams

WAR CRIES

As the war machine shifts into gear,
Mothers' children flee in fear
From promises, it won't happen here
Though once again, they lied.
The soldiers' once triumphant cry,
Lies buried, in the sand.

The guns of arrogance and pride,
Rage through the months from side to side,
Till there's no place for them to hide,
And no place to call home.
No God, to pray to end it all.
Heartbroken now 'he's' gone.

A wife, a mother, sits at home,
Her heart primed ready, by the phone.
Waiting; has he lost or won?
Willing him to survive.
While piece by piece, she dies herself
To keep her son alive.

Ian Robertson

SOUL ANALYSIS

To stimulate the imagination
To excite and enchant the soul,
To make us reach for and finally grab,
Our ambitions, our highest of goals.

To touch where we've never had feeling,
To grasp what we never could hold,
To fill us all with wonder and pride,
So we stand tall majestic and bold.

Let your body rejoice within laughter,
Let your heart be content with its fill,
The key to all of our wishes and dreams,
Lies within us, it's what we call will!

To echo a radiant laughter,
To drown out the sorrows and woes,
These gifts everyone of us truly could find,
If we just listen out to our souls.

Maria Teresa Reed

DREAMS

What would we do if we could not dream
of all the things that might have been,
Is reality such a fragile thing
Like the gossamer of a mayfly's wing.

It's dreams that keep our spirits high
The things to come, the days gone by
Wrapped in our imagination
We live our lives in expectation.

Living each day or month or year
hoping that better days will appear,
Yet if we only stopped to look
Our dreams are like an open book

Each page a wish - a path well trodden
each chapter read - a thought forgotten
For like a book well read and treasured
Our dreams will give us so much pleasure.

So don't keep them locked away unseen
or toss them out as 'might have been'
For when we've time for reverie
Our dreams become our memories.

Elaine Tamblyn

RESPECT ...

Life has its own means of time!
Once a child, not a care in the world,
Play, sleep and eat the menu of the day.
       Now just a memory.
Through the hustle and bustle of a
       Faceless crowd walk I.
Destination still not known.
Wiser with age I take up life's gauntlet
       Known as 'employment'.

Life goes on . . .
Today, other persons carry the gauntlet
Behold, you still see a wise old man.
His wisdom is given for young to hear
        And act upon.
This service is free to all, who wish
        To listen
But remember, one day you will
        Change places
Then - listening day's gone . . .

J J Connolly

THROUGH A CHILD'S EYES

We borrow the world from our children
They make us appreciate life
They show us there's more to just living
Forget about troubles and strife.
They're confident, bold and not frightened
Fear comes with age, as you know
They march in with both eyes wide open
To places where adults won't go
Everything's right in the eyes of a child
Depression and worry don't exist
Even pain only lasts for a second
When the sore spot, by mother is kissed
They fascinate you with things that they do
Amaze you with things that they say
But, whenever you're tired, or feel a bit low
They're there, to brighten your day.
On days when you wish you were single
Still working, with money to spare
Remember, they're not kids forever
But your children will always be there.

Karann Bamber

GULP, GULP

He loves me; he truly loves me,
We have shared a whirlwind romance.
He depends on me; he'd be lost without me,
I send him into a trance.
He confides in me; he relies on me,
I am his only friend.
He consumes me; he osculates me,
The tender passion will never end.
He savours me; he lavishes me,
I bring him pools of delight.
He pampers me; he humours me,
I am always in his sight.

I invade him; I excite him,
He is a pathetic fool.
I abuse him; I capture him,
He is so vulnerable.
I incite him; I expose him,
A wild addiction for me.
I deceive him; I tempt him,
Yet he's too blind to see.
I tease him; I damage him,
He takes it in his stride.

I absorb him; I confuse him,
Successfully ruin his pride.
I poison him; I stain him,
He's at the end of his toll.
I dissolve him; I bury him,
As I am alcohol.

Su Kendall (15)

FOREVER WITH ME

Sunshine. Nothing but sunshine,
And a soft, cool breeze,
As I look towards your face,
And into your mind.
You're thinking, dreaming,
Drifting through thoughts,
Of the past, of tomorrow,
Maybe today.
Hopes and dreams reflected in your crystal distant eyes.
Relaxed. You are calm, quiet and warm.
And you are at peace with yourself, with others.
Nothing's wrong. It's better now, you're safe,
Now better off than you would have been yesterday.
Time. Time is non-existent to you now.
No deadlines, no rush, no hurry, no worries.
Just you, yourself and me.
Me. One of your family,
One of the closest to you.
Today. I can't say goodbye today.
I haven't yet been able to say it,
Nor tomorrow.
The sunshine becomes brighter,
I can see you now.
Forever here.
      Forever with me.

Emma Louise Nyman

THE OPINIONS OF ONE

Etched denials, stained on souls.
In turmoil, self destruct mode.
Frail remorse, life's on course.
A bitter pill, so sweet to swallow.
In grand esteem, and yet so hollow.
Split the atom, no tomorrow.
Consequence, spent, a life just lent.
Epitomise tears, shed for years.
To take a life, maybe no surprise.
What lurks deep behind, those shallow eyes.
Impulsive sneers, repulsive jeers.
Racked in doubt, in fear of peers.
And how weak, yet strong, belief's not wrong.
Time well spent, much to resent.
Collective, corrective, bemused and rejected.
Another day passes, for all the world's masses.
Patriotic, hypnotic, a gift we've all got it.
Repent, heavenly sent, many angers to vent.
In a snare as one stares at the
Darkness out there, that sparkles,
And flickers, as life starts, stops and jitters.
To new beginnings and sorry ends, of
Many endless foes and friends.
Conflicting stories of many past glories
The mimic, the mocking, the
Onslaught non stopping.
Peace so serene is ideal it would
Seem.

Paddy Berry

A DAY IN THE COUNTRY

I woke up this morning,
A new day was dawning,
I opened the window,
The fresh air to breathe in.

I look down on the fields, in the valley below,
Watch the wheat sway, in the cool winds that blow,
Flowers in bloom, birds on the wing,
This vista of beauty, it makes your heart sing.

Fields in neat squares, in all shades of green,
The cattle and sheep add life to the scene,
Farmhands toiling in the heat of the day,
Some harvesting grain, some gathering hay.

Hedgerows give shelter, to all kinds of creatures,
Birds, mice and insects, are part of the features,
Berries, wild flowers, in abundance all grow,
It's all part of nature, and life in full flow.

A stream winds its way, through the valley so deep,
The water so clear, a picture to keep,
In your mind, to remember when you're troubled and sad,
To our memories we turn, to make us feel glad.

The old village church, with its huge Norman tower,
The clock set in the middle, which chimes every hour,
Graves in the churchyard have stories to tell,
Of the people at rest there, and their fate that befell.

The 'Travellers Rest' is set by the old village green,
An apt name for an inn, and a sight to be seen,
When you're tired and thirsty, and your legs feel like lead,
Enjoy a tankard of ale, and for the night book a bed.
A day in the country is my idea of heaven,
I'll say goodbye now, I'm tired, and it's half past eleven.

T Shutt

POETESS

Seeking out that star so distant,
Vivid, yet from earth's view a vision of what is no more;
Existing though by pondering view made constant,
Giving an epitaph to the glory gone before
Of in space holding the moment vibrant.

Assessing and exploring, the obvious, the now,
To capture and preserve the precise reality
Or create and expose an alternative how;
By deepest understanding in every diversity
And to that purpose truly vow.

As a kestrel hovering, its face to the wind,
With eyes far seeing and foreseeing,
Distance, time, change of every kind;
Appraising all events and situations feeling
And so satisfied the distant view to find.

The past will be made alive by your address
And of nothing omit or defect of any part
And the present vast or minute, you will redress:
Even though not yet happened, it will not evade your heart,
All time pervading, O ghostly poetess.

Avril Ellison

COLD NIGHT

Oh, cold night. Where is
your day
The warmth of your sunshine
do you weep, are you sad?

Oh, cold night, can I make
you smile, and give you
comfort, from the touch of
my embrace?

Oh, cold night, do you feel
the empty whispers, from the
chasm of my mind that only
dawn can fill?

Oh, cold night, reach out and
touch, those embers of my heart,
and warm your empty soul with
my embrace. Turn your night
into day and fill your
world with sunshine.

Sylvia Arthurs

THE AFTERGLOW

Sitting in the cafeteria
Glowing senses heightened
This is the calm after the storm
Got one's breath back, elated and enlightened

In this cosy retreat
Quenching one's thirst as one is able
Then there's the missing hat . . . you smile
'Nice brown eyes across the table'.

This inner warmth, a total oneness
Unique, special
What dreams are made of,
      or the highest of heights reached if one was able
Your eyes sparkling, glimmering like the stars
Reflecting back across the table

So at ease and so warm
Defenceless as one without cares
Your presence, your smile, your glowing face
      is the centre of the universe

Treasured Warmth

V Wilson

MEMORIES

I was born in nineteen twenty one
I don't know where the years have gone
Lots of changes I have seen
As if some things have never been
No electricity when I was a lass
And nobody had much brass
Scrubbed flag floors, a bucket and brush
Outside toilet with no flush
Dad made toys from cotton reels
Trains he'd make, with bobbin wheels
We didn't have much money
He'd make us laugh with tales so funny
We had no slippers then to wear
And the floor was flagged and very bare
Icy feet and cold red toes
It was so cold nobody knows
We walked to school a mile or so
No use crying or making a fuss,
There was no taxi or little red bus,
Nothing for it we had to go
On the desk teacher kept a cane
If we were late we felt the pain
At four o'clock we were free
To hurry home for our tea
No electricity at dark of night
Up to bed by candlelight
We'd kneel by the bed a prayer to say
Thank you Lord for another day
Those days have long gone with
Lots of laughter and tears
Where have they gone all those years?
Time goes by on flashing wings
Memories are made of lots of things

Ethel Cheetham

ICE QUEEN

Ice queen,
cool, calm, organised.
Always a smile,
reliable, with it,
a woman in control.

Can't they see
the fire within?
The rising passion,
unquenched desire?
The chaos that waits
below the surface.
The panic that lurks
within the soul.

What do they see?
Dependable Claire,
a port in a storm,
methodical, plodding.
Can they see inside me
to know what I feel?
Will they guess my problems?
Would they love me then?

Ice queen,
reliable, caring,
keeping my secrets hidden still.
No chink will show in my fragile armour.
No sign will show of this troubled mind.
Not just for my friends
the calm exterior,
the control exists
to pacify my soul.

Evelyn James

EPITAPH FOR ROSEMARY

Seen the sun shine on Rosemary's window,
Re-illumination of a once shining light.
We are striving to reawaken that repressed feeling
that Rosemary so readily gave.

Thought I saw her standing by the bridge that night,
faint realisation of an endless shadow upon my mind.

Through the sunlight on Rosemary's window, beyond the glare.
Happiness surely awaits for all those who
cared for those touches of Rosemary's.

Wherever we travel, Rosemary's there,
Feeling her presence, Rosemary's all around,
New light shining on new ground.

Once again in times of darkness, light
will come from Rosemary's window,
to guide us, to help to unite us.

Remember Rosemary and no trials will tear us apart.
Daring that final conflict, through our longest day,
when all the world about us is in turmoil.

Remember to believe and there will be light at
the end of the tunnel.
Light from Rosemary's window.

K Bellamy

MY ENGLAND, MY ROSE

What has happened to you my beautiful rose,
Your petals they have faded,
Your stem has slowly wilted.
You once were so beautiful -
The envy of the garden.
You were the one who was admired
by all the flowers around.

Now you stand in the shadows
of the garden of life.
Those that once envied now are to be envied,
And those that once respected now stand in the light.
They have grown and blossomed with petals blooming,
While you stand, and fade, and wilt.

My England, my rose,
Will you ever return as the envy of the garden,
and take back the place that is rightfully yours?

Lindsey Holliday

SEARCHING

The answer lies
deep in your soul,
If you are one
If you are whole.
Look to the future
the light ahead,
Walk your own destiny
don't be lead.
For everyone answers
to their own deeds,
up or down
Wherever it leads.
Take heed and listen
to what I say,
it makes all the difference
on judgement day.

S Bradbury

DUNBLANE

An evil came to the town of Dunblane
With it came murder, sorrow and pain,
So many young innocents killed in cold blood.
With their teacher who showed
                          them nothing but good
We weep, we grieve with the town of Dunblane
And pray that they all may smile once again
Some time in the future, but surely not yet.
For this horror is something we'll never forget,
We send you our comfort and also our love
While your babies are resting with God up above
Your most precious gift, to him you had given.
For the children of Dunblane are the Angels of
                          Heaven.

Irene Dodd

ALL ALONE

I want so much to tell you all the things I never said
There are so many things that keep going through my head
Did I tell you how much I love you? No you never knew.
I could have made you so happy when you were feeling so blue
There are so very many things that I didn't say
Now you will never know my love, now you've gone away
I walk through the woods on a cold winter morn
my heart feels broken and oh so torn
For my love she has gone and now I'm alone
feeling as though I'm made of stone
Oh come back my love let us try once more
my life will begin again when you walk through the door

G Wells

MOTHER EARTH

I can remember when the world was bright,
flourishing with the sun's unearthly light.
When trees and plants covered the land.
A resting place for birds to land.
Seasons cold and hot they came
though predictable, but never the same.
Animals wandering through the grass,
a safe haven from the predators that pass.
Fish and coral adorned the sea,
but now some say, 'What could that be?'
It is alas the sea.
What was adorned with beauty,
has now collected the world's not wanted booty.
Huge ash clouds blot out the light,
darkness is here, what a sight.
Chimneys pouring out poisonous smog.
People dying, choking, gasping help!
Trees are gone, nothing can survive,
birds and creatures aren't alive.
Nothing breathes the world is dead.
Black as black, ash and dust
polluted and toxic, trash and muck.
Rivers gone, sludge remains.
People live in fear and disease among
the rats, and in the drains.

This could be your future

Richard Kirchin (13)

REVELATION

So you know my mind?
Aah! You stole in through my eyes,
Portals to my cavernous interior.
You used your guile,
Tempted my secrets out of their
Dark hiding places,
Like bats, seduced by the promise of
Succulent moths.
You saw those things didn't you?
The images I meant to destroy.
I tried! I really did!
They just wouldn't catch light,
Though I held a flame
To their ragged corners for an age.

Graham R Bell

GOODBYE MY LOVE

No longer shall I see your sweet face before I close my eyes.
Nor shall I hear your gentle voice saying, hurry don't be late.
No longer shall I return to a welcoming light.

Nor shall I fill a shopping basket with food for two or shout
'bye my sweet darling I do love you'.

The time did come, as we knew it would
and you said goodbye,
then I made a promise
to love you until the day I die.

Now your soul has flown in search of paradise,
but my love, I did not have time to say thank you for
leaving me something to cherish until the day I die.

Heidi Chalfont

THE BOOKMARK
(Written after the death of our son, John)

I was feeling broken hearted and deep sobs did rack my breast
I thought of many good things but from grief I found no rest
My loved one watched me with concern and he shared my pain
All his words of comfort were lost and so in vain
I climbed the stairs and in my room
A bookmark lay on the floor
It said a prayer can bring relief
From pain, from grief and more
I knelt there in the solitude and prayed dear God above
Help me with this awful pain, look down on me with love
My words they must have drifted behind great heaven's door
For whilst I was praying I felt calm right to my core
My body felt like sunlight came after heavy rain
And I felt laughter grow in me as I spoke my Master's name
My heart felt so much lighter - the pain had eased away
I thanked my Father warmly and then went on my way
The laughter stayed within me like a sweet refreshing breeze
And my loved one he was happy to see me so at ease
The pain it comes and goes on still
But I know we're not alone
For God is on the hills and fields and also in our homes
Do you have a heartache
Speak to Him tonight
And brothers and sisters, please believe
He will put it right.

Margaret Scott

THE DESTROYER

I watch as people innocently walk,
Walk into my outstretched arms,
Life is snuffed out,
Like a candle in the wind,
I am the destroyer,
I devour pain.
The agony of others,
is my saviour,
I am the darkness,
Solitude beckons me,
I walk on,
Alone.

Emma Boolaky

SEARCHING

I search and search inside and out
But it seems I cannot find
The prize that's there without a doubt
I think they call it peace of mind
As I sit beneath this old oak tree
How wise it looks and grand
My face it cools to the breeze
And I melt into the land.
I wonder is this what I long for
The calmness I can't find
Maybe, I need look no more
Is this it, that peace of mind

But all too soon the calmness goes
And my mind it fills again
Through my body the confusion flaws
It seems I must live with the pain.

N Coleman

POWER OF ONE

Seventy-five thousand silenced by the knowledge,
Of sixteen little voices screaming.
It makes me feel,
So incredibly small,
To realise the *power of one*.

You cannot justify an action,
So mind-numbingly wrong.
It's not easy to understand,
How just a singular man,
Can manipulate the *power of one*.

How the day stops for just a minute,
How the World is so incredibly still.
Yet why should it take,
Such a fatal mistake,
To demonstrate the *power of one*.

It's not right, it's not clear,
There is no just cause,
To bring everyone here.
Yet the World keeps turning,
Angry words will keep burning,
In sympathetic ears.

How every Mother's heart is chilled,
At the action of one individual,
And the *power of one*,
As he points the gun.

We could talk for years, trying to explain,
About whatever happened that day,
Nothing could ever reconcile Dunblane,
Only time can wash the tears away.

Kathryn Louise Jordin

THE SUNSET

As I gaze from my window
The sight that meets my eyes
The colours and the shades
Lighting up the skies
There's red, grey and blue
To mention just a few
How they intermingle
Giving such a view,
The mountains of Scotland
Silhouetting on the sea
The gulls are flying high and low
Hoping for a catch
In the distance a fishing boat
To collect its latest batch.
These sights are the Solway
For all to come and see
The spirit and the calm
The tranquillity.

J Lawson

A PLEA

Take me safely back to shore
Protect me from the wind
The rain
The dark deep pools of pain
Protect me from the hidden rocks
The waves, the shocks
Of reality -
Please, I ask no more
Take me safely back to shore

Sandra M Leggat

HOUSE ON THE HILL

Standing
    as a old house
Stoic
    seperate on a hill
Window shades drawn
Your eyes   no entry
              no sunlight here

The door . . . locked
        warped
          heavy oak

intriguing to me what others pass without a glance

or turn from . . . convinced of vacancy

But there is a tenant here
a soul lives . . . beyond
        the neglected
           lace curtains

hide from view

A treasure

am I alone in my perception

With no hesitation; for fear of loss I scale the hill
    slowly
        calculated
            so as not to disturb
                Its sentinel . . .
                    Fear

Helena Strauss

PAST TIME

Another second passes,
Always to precede
Time is so precious
Time is all you need
Gone as leaves in autumn time,
Yet never to return.
True, green will grow again
But people never learn
A special gift, stolen away,
Nowhere to be found
Days and weeks pass by,
Knowing the end is bound
'Just one more minute'
Is a well known cry
But however much we beg and plead
The time still passes by.
But how slowly do the hands move,
When time is in reverse.
A pace so slow and dreary,
That seems to hold a curse.
But time is made for sharing,
However long and short.
Please use your time wisely
As more can not be bought!

Emily Sissons (16)

A SHEDDED TEAR

A shedded tear
The drop of rain
A silent whisper
The sweet breeze
A budding rose
The new life
A summer's day
The smile of laughter.

A gentle touch
The feather drops
A magic path
The map of life
A broken heart
The thorn of pain
        A shedded tear,
           The drop of rain.

J Macleod

MY PRIVATE HELL

As the pain grips me darkness falls,
I am in my own private hell.
What have I done to deserve this?
Through screams and tears I feel I have no control,
The pain is too great to bear.
It controls my life and destroys my state of mind.
I feel death is my only escape, but I cannot
              let it win
Nothing helps as it takes over my body.
I cannot sit or stand.
My screams show the outside world part of my anguish.
I know it will be over soon, but what about the next time?
When will they take me seriously and cure me of this hell?
3 years have passed and I feel I cannot continue.
Why should I?
I dread next month as I do not know what it has in store for
              me.
I feel I have suffered enough.
Life is unfair.
Help me someone, please take away my pain.
Before I put an end to it myself.
I do not wish to die, but with this pain I cannot live.

Nicola Watton

TRAVEL BROADENS THE HEART

Through my life's path I seem to find
I choose too often the wrong track
Then to the start I must go back

So many bridges have been crossed
Needlessly with unfounded fears
Oh what a waste of precious years

My higher self at last gained sway
'Dear child to travel is an art
Direct yourself more with the heart

What is this journey all about
If not to help the spirit grow
Teaching new things needed to know

Go dice with chance - try the untried
The safe option's not always wise
For it can be the coward's guise

Drop fast those reins holding you tight
Let inner courage be your guide
'Twill be a much less bumpy ride

Secrets buried deep far too long
Will then direct you from the soul
Helping you reach your destined goal'

It took me long - but no regrets
Experience has shown me how
To travel best life's journey now

Tina Lipman

O DEATH (LIFE BEFORE DEATH)

O death, you are both old and wise,
What have you seen with your sightless eyes?
Many have gone with you to the grave,
Kings and the poor, meek and the brave.
O death, in your bones you hold the sweet release,
Your scythe takes both man and beast.

O friendless death,
Ancient death,
The one who walks both sides.
O ruthless death,
Tireless death,
What is it your cloak hides?

A family, a wife, a life from ancient time?
A love of flowers, of romance, or literature and rhyme?
There must have been something before all this,
Something that brought relief and bliss.
Tell me Lord Reaper, before you knight my head,
What brought you to this dark bed?

O sad death,
Lustful death,
Have you a soul?
O beautiful death,
Blood stained death,
What made you take this role?

Paul Colbourne

FEELINGS AND THOUGHTS

A certain kind of sadness is with me all through the year.
Thinking of my mum 'the best' I wish that she was still here.
People say you get over it. I know it isn't true.
The ache just goes a little less, but it still stays with you.

The Christmas time is coming, it's coming a little too fast.
All that I can think about is the good ones in the past.
As I close my curtains and look up at the sky lights
I'm really hoping that you are the star that's shining bright.

My little boys' faces shine, their eyes light up with glee.
All their lovely presents suit them to a tee.
They stand around the Christmas tree, and sing so very proud,
I believe that you can see them mum, but I wish you were still around.

A lot will have these thoughts at this time of year.
And where there's lots of happiness, there's also lots of tears.
So Merry Christmas, a wave, a bit of Christmas cheer.
To a friend and even a stranger, they could be missing someone dear.

E Banks

MILLENNIUM'S END

Under a blood red moon
A dark iron railed balcony,
Sounds of the city rise
Out of the neon enhanced darkness.

Tonight my love we need no sleep
For tonight we feed in the metropolis.
Drinking in the brazen opulence
Of the Parisianesque costume dramas,
Unfolding in the time of judgement.

For now these undeveloped worlds collide
In synchronous orbits at this millennium's end,
And it is time to dance and cavort to excess.
Amongst these mortal hedonist fantasies
Flushed with faces that perceive no fear.
As we spread and propagate that trepidation
On guilt-edged wings of religious fever.
For this is the end of their time
And the beginning of ours.

Chris Goodrum

NAN

I remember all the happy days
There was joy for you and me
Time never can erase the thoughts
We can share in memory

You held that special kindness
Showing deepest thoughts and fears
But your soul was like a beacon
When your eyes were dim with tears

My mind recalls the distant past
I smell your cooking and perfume
The patter of your tiny feet
Still echoes through the room

We cannot change life's destiny
It holds nothing that will last
Life only is a pathway
Strewn with memories of the past

Gill Hewett

LOOKING ACROSS TO THE ISLAND

Look across the water . . the mist
Hides the island
The water is calm, except for
Geese swaying up and down
The odd screech from the gulls
A scream that demands
Oh sun shine through the mist and
Let me see the island's crown,
Horizons, far, far across,
Small hills merging with forest and fields
At last, the sunshine breaks and yields
Making sparkling stars of grey seas
And I smile to myself and think of yesterday.

Rosie Webster

LIFE GOES ON

Another day goes by, slowly and still,
Another child is born, but what will that life bring?
Nothing left for anyone to do,
No work, no money, who's at fault who?
Is it ourselves, is it the government?
I wish I knew.
Watching folk daily their faces so blue,
What's happened to this town it used to be great,
Till the factories and pits closed, it sealed our fate.
Sometimes I wish I had royal blood
Nothing to worry about plenty of money and food,
But alas I'm just me, simple and plain,
There's lots like me, we're all the same.
It's not our fault but tell me who's to blame?
Until we find out, we'll have to live with the shame.

Susan Hansen

AUTUMN

Autumn - season of mists and mellow sneezes
No more summer breezes
Summer flies behind
No more sunbathes to unwind
Why did it go so quick?
Why is this morning's fog so thick?
Put the summer clothes away
Prepare for moths, buy a spray
Look ahead, long dark days
Christmas coming, hopes to raise
Christmas coming, money to raise
Forget Christmas, take an autumn break
Read the brochures, keep awake
Majorca, Tenerife, Caribbean, Spain
Somewhere where there is no rain
No rain, no cold, no dark, just sun
Pack the bags, all abroad have fun
Gotta come back raise some cash
Gotta come back face the splash
Is it all in the mind?
Do we need the sun to unwind?
Think ahead, not long till next year
Dry your eye, don't shed a tear
Think ahead, not long till next summer
Think ahead, do a runner
Some have the choice, some have the cash
Some dare do something rash
Take the plunge, to yourself be kind
Travel only broadens the mind

Linda Tongue

JOY OF CONVERSATION

I tried so hard to light her life;
Told tales to bring forth smiles.
I talked of fun, gossip and strife.
She talked about her piles.

I thought I'd turn to current news,
The latest burning question.
I said I'd love to hear her views.
She talked of indigestion.

I chattered of the film I'd seen;
Of houses underpinned;
Of every topic there has been.
She talked about her wind.

I praised her little grandson so
(To turn the conversation) -
That perfect nose! That dinky toe!
She talked of constipation.

I did try hard to keep a grin
And hide reactions drear,
And only turned the whole thing in
When she got to diarrhoea.

C Baxter

LIFE OF DREAMS

This is the end of my life of dreams,
my life that was woven in pain,
for love's not as real as it first seems,
and the heartaches always remain.

I've stood at the cross-roads of death only twice,
and changed my mind at the last,
for they say third time lucky and this is twice,
for I can never forget the past,

If I had someone to talk to
then maybe I could find a future,
once I had hope but I have no one to talk to you see,
and all I can do is to cry and mope,

I wish I could forget him and God I do try,
it's getting so bad I feel ill,
they're pulling me down all these tears that I cry,
oh my darling how I love you still.

E Robson

LONG DAYS

Bright tongues of fire crackled in the grate,
The room was quiet and peaceful,
As if lying in wait.
The day was at long last over,
The night held no fear.
After what had gone before,
Now was the time to hold memories dear.

Memories of times so long ago,
Of happiness and joy, to be kept in store.
When each day held a promise of pleasures to come,
Most are all gone now, forgotten by some.

That day she left everything changed,
Nothing was ever to be the same.
All that was left to pass the hours
Was everyone wondering just who was to blame.

Where is she now, is she hiding in pain?
The hearts left behind bleeding as if slain.
Broken in two though fickle and weak,
The truth is out there, the quest is to seek.

Ina Howes

NEVER WE SEE

This road has a fork
Which way do we go?
In the darkness we walk
Do you hear
  your shadow talk?

Never we see
All that happens
Behind the scenes
Within our dreams
Ignorance - your mind runs free

This path we do take
Our hands, they are holding
Destiny
Our future unfolding

Never we see
All that happens
Behind the scenes
Within our dreams
Ignorance - your heart is free

We're not alone
The time we waste
Where have we gone?
What have we done?
The things we chased

Never we see
All that happens
Behind the scenes
Within our dreams
Ignorance - your conscience free

But are you . . . are you free?

R J Fowler

YOU'RE NOT A VICTIM YOU'RE A SURVIVOR

In your own little world are you locked up inside
Do you sometimes feel you'll go right out of your mind
Does your life seem to be getting you down
Then don't sit there pondering and wearing that frown
As you feel your life is trapped in a big steel cage
And your life is a book with a missing last page
The key to your cage is locked up deep inside
Yet looking for that key makes you want to hide
The missing page of your book is deep in your heart
And looking for that page is tearing you apart
But that outstretched arm of help is really there for you
Take hold of that arm is all you have to do
Not reaching out for that arm just won't do at all
There's always someone there to listen so just give them a call
The first steps are the hardest that much I know
But you're not a victim you're a survivor be proud and let it show.

June Hierons

CAROUSEL

Let's take a ride on the old carousel
A timeless rotation the children love well
Mounted high on horseback clasp tightly the reins
Our elegant journey glides in orbital lanes
All around faces merging and voices are blending
Distant trees become moving seas a kaleidoscope never ending
As In Queen Victoria's and now Elizabeth's time
The same accordion melody plays its antique rhyme
Yet swifter and higher the stallions leap
A Grand National of colour to elation we reach
Then carousel slows back to reality
We dismount breathless with excitement and in calamity
Always we remember this majestic dome
Where through dimensions of decades children can roam

E A Heywood

TUESDAY MIDNIGHT - CUDDLEOMETER ON FULL - SIPPING SECOND MUG OF TEA AS PRESCRIBED

What are these threads that hold us
Are your threads the same as mine
The webs as fine as gold dust
Are beginning to entwine

Do you feel the same attraction
Of magnetic force begin
To act upon a fraction
Of your being - pull you in

Does a magnet in each other
Pull so gently, far away
Then approaching close, take over
Cataclysmic force display

There is one north - one south pole
Equator in between
And the parts strive to make one whole
Though the power remains unseen

We rotate around in tandem
Gravitation is displayed
What will trigger off the random
Pull that springs the trap we made

When the force locks us together
With inseparable strength
There could be a shattering tremor
Felt at universal length

    12.30 Time for another tea

Garth

STEREOTYPES

Whatever was I doing
That was so very wrong
You told me to stop
I wanted to carry on
You shouted at me
And called mc names
The object of your hate
You said I was to blame
You threatened me
And grabbed me in your rage
An outcast of society
That should be in a cage
Your small-minded prejudices
Fill my mouth with distaste
A healthy human brain
Going to enormous waste

Alison Tilley

HIDDEN DEPTHS!

Oh! Thou dark satanic river,
That I gaze upon with awe.
What evil lies beneath that calm exterior
That thy wicked soul doth hide -
Ravaged by forces unseen,
Silently ebbing and flowing
Condemning me as I stroll along in anger
My mood as dark and brooding,
As the clouds looking down in fury
Like drawn curtains across my face.
Ripples slowly widening as they calm a soul
        Tormented by hate!
A breast beating wild with passion,
And emotions hitherto unknown . . .

Freda F Ringrose

IN TWENTIES KENT

Where I was born
Golden fields of waving corn
Orchard blossoms
Of pink and white
Heaven sent - a lovely sight
Hop gardens
What fun we had
Riding on the farmer's nag
School holidays came
And freed from class
Camping we went on Romney Marsh
What times we had
In those far off days
Ne'er will we see their like again
I've wandered far o'er land and sea
But my heart will ever be
Where my family long
Have lingered
In the lovely
Garden of England

William G Hackney

FICKLE EMOTIONS

Like a warm summer breeze
A tender kiss sweeps over me
Emotions slowly swell within
Craving liberty.

Hues of smoky purple haze
Swirl around subconscious thoughts,
As kisses melt increasing doubts
And worries wrought.

Colours of a vivid hue,
Bursting, blundering uncontrolled.
Fiery feelings seemingly
Forever taking hold.

Passion finally unfolded
Into peaceful, tranquil mood,
Remnants of ebbing emotions
Quietly subdued.

Christine Barrow

A SPECIAL SOMEONE

When I need someone to share my thoughts
There is a heart that understands
When I seek the warmth of a comforting touch
There are welcome outstretched hands
When I need someone close to me
Someone who will really care
Your heart and your hands reach out in love
And I'm happy to know you are there
Someone with a smile so warm
And a heart so kind and good
That words are not always needed
For so much is understood
I need someone very special
To depend on come what may
And because you are that someone
You bring loving thoughts my way
How wonderful it is to know
There is someone always there
Who really wants to listen
And to understand and care.

Margaret Ford

YORKSHIRE HERITAGE

I tread the wide, wild moor, where windswept purple heather
Clings tenaciously to contoured earth.
My heaving lungs, for I am old, savour the good clean moorland air.
A startled, feathered form breaks cover at my tread, it's
Lagging fellows join, to soar aloft.
The flock departs beyond the hill to rest again perhaps, ere
Comes another alien step.
The summer's colouring beyond, is yet one facet to the wholesome
Scene. The patchwork fields, the drystone walls, the farmer's
Cot so neat. The hedgerows teeming full of life, the scudding
Clouds, the trees.

Alas! Euphoria begins to wane, I look, and look again beyond
This pastoral Shangri-la.
Is that a vapour trail I see far above the clouds? There's
Another, and another. Each trail, a silver, human cargo laden
Monster at its head, a different aerial pathway takes;
And breaks the spell.

I further look upon this suddenly contrasting scene, to see a pylon
Bearing ugly wires. The gyrations of a stark, tall, hungry
Wind generator beside a scarred and quarried hill, seek to
Distract my floating mind. I stumble on my eroded pathway,
Which, widened and crumbled by mountain bike and a million
Tourist boots, steers me to my next sad site, the picnic spot,
Complete with motor car and litter in this haven on the moor.

My sojourn into past, so brief, now fades. Disillusioned, I retrace my steps,
The tower blocks of Keighley come to view, the spell completely
Broken now.
I weep;
  For this Haworth Moor where Brontë children walked,
    And breathed, and dreamed.

Geoff Bowden

PRECIOUS MOMENTS

A glimpse of heaven in a rainbow
A sunset moment we can share
The first cry of a baby
The cherished words 'I care'
The moment when your wish comes true
When you doubted far too long

The pleasure of a friendship
The joy of love in a song
The sudden song of a skylark
As it rises up so high
The soothing sound the river makes
As it goes gurgling by

The caressing warmth of the summer sun
That strokes you into sleep
The fleeting glimpse of a butterfly
That's too beautiful to keep
The tender touch of a loved one
As you hold each other's hand

What more can life envisage
We know that all was planned
How can we then not marvel
At all things great and small
The cricket and the grasshopper
The trees so strong and tall

These all are precious moments
We live with and enjoy
Each with its special message
Of beauty that does not cloy . . .

V M Coote

MOTHER

A mother's love is forever free,
And full of things that like to be,
Getting cross and angry along the way;
Are stepping stones towards the day
When out in the wide world we go
Remembering all the things we should know,
But mother, this special note
Sums everything up that should be said,
You are very special and I will always hold
The highest candle I could find,
You are in my thoughts daily and should be told;
I would like to be like you, of that special mould
Mother you mean so much more
More than words can ever say
But I just thank you from the heart
For being my mother, and playing that part.

Margaret McQuilton-Morgan

WHERE

Where do you go when things go wrong
What do you do, when not so strong
How can you feel, when feeling's not there
How can you look, when there's only despair

Where are the answers? Where is the hope?
Where is that rainbow? Where is the gold?
Searching, searching, is all that you do
Searching for what . . . you haven't a clue

The solution is there. You know! You can hear it
Just one more grasp, and then you will feel it
Reach! Reach! You are just about there
Another wall! You can but stare

Angela Morton

GOLDEN YEARS

A lonely table, set for tea - one cup, one plate, there's only me,
  Resting, with the day's work done, watching, as the setting sun
Casts golden light upon the wall; waiting, till the soft rays fall
  Upon the pictures hanging there, rich with colour, fresh and fair.

No ordinary pictures these, painted views, the eye to please,
  But scenes we knew, and loved so much, held forever by the touch
Of skilful hands, each coloured stitch, our life reliving, warm and rich.
  The blue of lochs, so clear and deep; white for clouds, and rain-washed
                                                                                sheep;
Purple, for the Scottish heather; grey, the rocks we climbed together.
  Rowan red, and chestnut brown; soft green, the rolling English Down.
And gold, for golden years I treasure, filled with love no words can measure.

Each well-known scene, each spray of flowers, a memory holds of pleasant
                                                                                 hours;
  Companionship, no pain can sever, though you, my dear, are gone forever.
A loved one lost, so young and fair, brought sorrow, more than you could
                                                                                  bear -
  Your gentle heart was torn with pain, you neither spoke, nor walked again
And hands that held such patient skill, alas, for evermore lay still.

No last farewell could e'er be spoken, no touch of hand in grateful token;
  No loving smile could light your eye, to softly chide me, should I sigh.
But though of speech and sight bereft, a legacy of joy you left,
  And every room your presence knows, your love in every colour glows.
This very cloth I lay for tea, was one you worked on, just for me,
  And as I smooth each silken fold, this truth, I know, 'twill ever hold -
One cup, one plate, a single chair - yet not alone, for you are there.

Iris Ruthven

MOUNTAINS

As I gaze upon these mountains -
all around me here.
Which remind me of the good Lord -
who spent days and nights, alone in -
prayer, for people like you and me.
And upon that other hill called -
Golgotha, He shed His blood for -
a world sick with sin.
My! What love He showed the world.
And if these mountains here, remind
me of things such as these
We shall always be kept in mind -
of the good Lord, and what He did -
for you and me. All because He -
loved us so
It was a heavenly Father love, that -
caused Him to send His beloved son -
down to earth, to show us the way -
for us to live by faith alone.
David of old, liked the mountains -
to gaze upon their peaks, because -
it reminded him, of the good Lord
in glory and of His power everywhere.

N B Mason

DREAMS

With love in my heart.
I dream of you.
Hoping you are thinking of me too.

With love in my heart.
I love you so.
Hoping that you love
me also.

With love in my heart.
I wish to hold you in my arms.
Hoping you will return.
My love charms.

With love in my heart.
I know this can never be.
For I only love you
in my dreams.

Peter Fowler

THE SUNSET

The copper sphere, the jewel of day
Dripped jaded but golden from our sight
And left the land coated with rays
Of the most purest amber light;
And the soft breeze did gently play
Upon the sleeping face of night.

Silver stars slipped into the skies,
Their light entwined with the sun's soft glow;
And upon this horizon lies
Silhouettes which hold the deep unknown.
And the pale beams of crimson shines
Onto the world where night is thrown.

The placid ambience suspends still
On fragile threads above our land,
Untouched by all creatures shrill
And can't be touched by wicked hands.
Unharmed by the wind's bitter chill
This sunset dies and the day is fulfilled.

Kate Hewitt

MESSAGE

When you're living out on the street
You haven't really got the time to sleep
Your scared of getting stabbed or hit
As a bottle of beer you lay and sip
Your mind's away in a constant daze
And the local streets are a violent maze
Spinning around inside your head
And a concrete path is your only bed
You would steal anything just to get a fix
But drugs and life you know don't mix
You inject the pain into your brain
You see the world in another domain
You fall asleep but you don't wake
'Cause it was an OD that you did take
Nobody asks if you were seen
This is real life it isn't a dream
Life goes on without you there
There's no one left to say a prayer
Here one minute and the next you're gone
And is this right or is it wrong
There's not much more for me to say
I gotta get by from day to day
But I hope sometime that you will see
That this was your message from me

Gary Stewart

TRANQUILLITY

We slept by the hillside so peaceful and green
Not a person nor a vehicle there was to be seen
Our company consisted of the birds and the frogs
And occasionally interspersed with a couple of dogs.

Isn't it sad and more so a pity
That we cannot share it with kids from a city.
Their lives are so full of video and TV
They really don't know that 'tis like heaven to be
Away from the rat-race with only nature to see.

So let us drink up and our cup overfill,
From this corner of England so quiet and tranquil.

D Mary Cross

NO TIME TO SAY GOODBYE

We never said 'Goodbye'
For how could we have known
That tragedy would overrule
Plans made by telephone?

Our friendship, spanning 50 years
Was 'special' and unique
Surviving war
And so much more
But yet, within the week -
I learned of your collapse and death
It was quite beyond belief -
Ten weeks before, when my husband died
You had helped me through my grief.

So, who can help me now, dear friend,
As I sigh and wonder why
Those we love
Depart so quick
With no time to say 'Goodbye.'

Doreen Conway-Haynes

DEATH AND WAR

It's just as if you know
That your time to go is near
You wonder constantly what it is like
You wonder, and wonder, and wonder.
Questions pass through your mind
When will they ever be answered?
Of course you know when this will be -
When you arrive, and you can see.
Do we pass into another life?
Or simply stay behind forever?
The answers are known only
By those who've gone into those unknown realms -
They know what's there - for they have seen.
Who knows what will happen
So many questions - so little time?
It doesn't have to be like that
Make the most of what you have -
Just do the best of what you can.
Death and war, war and death,
Both hold certain risks
We know that they are inextricably linked
and will be until eternity.
The fear of death can be overcome
for surely it is peaceful?
And war can be diminished
or is there no chance of harmony and friendship?
We all have fears, we all have worries -
They nudge us at the back of our minds.
But if we unite and hold together
we are as one for ever and ever.

Helen Jackson

A MISSING LIGHT

My heart is broken
Since you went away,
I think of you often,
Both night and day.
You have your youth,
You will always keep,
I'll have old age,
And still shall weep.

You stand so tall,
Big and strong.
If only you could have stayed,
Where you belong.
But our thoughts will never go away.
For we shall all be together some day.

Julie Ovington

HOW I FEEL

Nobody knows how the pain feels inside.
The screaming and crying you're sure you must hide.
People who love you think you feel fine,
but that's what's in their heads, not what's in mine.
I feel the loneliness, I feel the distress, noboby knows
that I feel such a mess.
How I feel doesn't matter to me,
I locked myself away and I lost the key.
I cannot change for there's too much to heal,
this is my life and it's how I feel.

Amy Carrigan

A WHISPERED CARESS

There is a special garden,
That grows within my heart.
The flowers from tiny seeds were sown,
Each one a message to impart.

One called forget-me-not,
And with the morning sun,
Spreads its tiny petals and whispers,
A new day has begun.

A deep red rose, a rose called love.
Caresses my heartstrings, like the wings of a dove,
You will always be there in my garden to share,
The sweet scented flowers, that blossom with care.

These are my memories, but still they live on,
In my special garden, although you are gone.

Hilda Hindle

I SAW THE MERMAID BURN

I saw the mermaid burn
As I sat cross legged
On the sea front wall.
Her hair once as black as sleep
A cascade of flames
Tonguing at her side.
The pit black pupils of her eyes
Searching me out
Through the heated shimmering air.
Her incendiary ocean blackening
And ascending as ash,
Until all that remains
Are her framed horizons,
Scorched into memory.

Lloyd Richards

THE SEPARATION

A shattered life
A broken heart
The darkest hour
Now we are apart.

A fragment of a smile
At a wonderful memory
A sea full of tears
At what was meant to be.

A lifetime of dreams
Of what was before
Embracing my mind
Until we meet once more.

I think of love, I ache, I cry
I sit and gaze up at the sky
I watch the clouds and drops of rain
While you walk with angels and feel no more pain.

Tracy Roberts

FUTILITY

To build up a city, then blow it away
Having a baby that cries every day,
Giving a life full of anger and pain,
Trying to show it's worth living again,

A face at a window, begging for food,
You can plead all you like it won't do any good,
The food has all gone to a greedier man,
Who grows fat on the sweat of your sons.

Pauline Hill

THE ORCHARD

People here in peace sublime,
Contemplating with peace of mind
More than ever, here to say
Of joy at Brooke's and Russel's way.

Cambridge sky, blue again,
Orchard blossoms wash away the pains,
Granta in the distance flows,
Carries away their cares and woes.

Its path through meadows, ancient green,
Flows onwards, ever serene
For hundreds of years people have walked along
These tranquil waters, reflecting times gone.

The birds sweet song carries through the trees,
The buzzing bee in gentle breeze,
Blossoms of pink and apple white,
Move gently at the day's delight.

But time for me to move away,
Leaving the orchard to those who may,
Contemplate their own thoughts, desires,
For me, as with Brookes, the place never tires.

So along the path, brushing trees soft branches,
I wend my way to take my chances,
With the wider world outside this place,
To a real world? . . . A faster pace.

How times have changed over the years,
Life has brought us laughter and tears,
So why must I leave this place so serene,
Amongst the blossoms and trees so green?

Life is why and must evermore,
But I'll return whenever I may, to seek the joy of Brooke's and Russel's way.

Kevin Hard

1919

The cenotaph had been unveiled beside the village square,
Its ordered ranks of names engraved with sympathetic care.
Now it stands for all to see - solemn, sombre, stern,
Commemorating those who left, never to return.
But many men who had returned had not remained complete,
Missing either arms or legs, eyes or hands or feet.
Others carried subtle wounds of a different kind,
Shell-shocked, they could not escape the terrors of the mind.
Civilians too had paid a price, with many loved ones lost,
All were victims of the war, waged at fearful cost.
There was no doubt that it had been a truly worthy cause,
Newspapers had called it the war to end all wars.
Now, with peace restored at last, the war being newly won.
Who could know, in twenty years, there'd be another one . . .

F Jensen

THROUGH MY WINDOW

As I look out my window there's fields all around,
Horses galloping about without a sound,
It's so quiet peaceful and still,
As I look out the window with my arms on the sill,
The birds are singing a happy tune,
I'll hear the children in the playground soon,
An aeroplane flies by,
As I hear a baby cry,
But it's still so quiet peaceful and still,
As I look out the window with my arms on the sill.

L Corke

TO THE DEAREST OF THE DEAR

The undying love of one's heart,
Has brought me afar to be with thee,
Time and patience has made me the wiser;
You are my true love,
My sweet heart!

Your lamb-like qualities are impeccable,
Your fair visage is indescribable.

I can only portray thee,
Next to a blossoming scarlet rose,
Whose face is as soft as velvet,
And whose fragrance is as fresh and sweet,
As the morning dew,
On a midsummer's morn.

Your eyes glisten in the sun,
Like dazzling white sand on a tranquil beach.

Your nose, your lips,
Your ears, your hair,
All of which are inaccessible,
To the poor soul who begs thee.
But you fair maiden, you are the lock,
And me: I am the key.

For only together may we unlock
Each other's everlasting love,
Of eternity.

Francis Dias

METEORITE DELIGHT

If they should discover there's life on Mars
After finding micro-fossils in a meteorite
Would mad professors swoon with delight
And would Bowie be playing in disco bars

Would William Hill refuse to pay a dime
On bets that were laid in a previous time.
Would they cut the odds from a zillion to one
On the chance of finding ice-cream in the sun

Would Thomas Cook accept an early booking
From Earth to Mars, to go microbe looking
Could it be, two adults and one child free
Or will it be long haul at a premium fee

Would estate agents travel on the first flight
Waving sales brochures of Martian delight
Estates full of houses, built just for two
Typically Martian with lovely Earth view

Would the taxman soon be there
To impose a tax on Martian air
Forcing new Martians to pay their due
To the Interplanetary Revenue

Would they discover the red was mere dust
A covering for Mars a secretive crust
Concealing a treasure none could see
A blue precious world, Lapis Lazuli

Would an atmosphere bring changes there
A song in the rain for all to share
The rain the sun and stormy weather
A world with a coat of purple heather

Adrian Stafford

WINTERTIDE

The silence of the night is stirred
By strong pulses from the north that
Cut across the moonlit ocean
The waters shimmer and gleam like gold
As nature begins its perpetual motion

An increased volume of sound greets the land
And the hooting of an owl
Fading away into the hills
Is replaced by the breath
Of mother nature's icy chills

In a lonely dwelling in a distant field
The mice, they scurry across the beams
Quickly seeking a place to rest
In the sanctuary of their straw clad nests

Fir trees in a forest glade, bow down
And quiver, as the majestic force of life rises
Across its streams and rivers
Down, through the valleys, the villages and towns
The windsong continues until at last
The silence of the night abounds
Snowflakes are falling without a sound

Michael Monaghan

REBIRTH

Today I feel that I've been born
I see peace before my eyes
The calmness of the gurgling brook
As it ripples slowly by
The hue of greens and ambers
Strewn around me at my feet
All combine to make my birthplace
So peaceful and complete

Watching massive oaks and ashes
Sway in rhythm with the wind
The innocent young rabbits
As they play amongst the heath
And as I look above me
Woolly clouds go flitting past
Midst the azure of their background
I'm glad I've arrived at last.

Doreen H M Scott

MORE BAD NEWS

I switch on the television
To watch the latest news.
I sit in my favourite armchair
To get the best views.
The news is bad
Full of gloom
I turn it off
And I leave the room.
Then I hear sirens
There's a blue flashing light
As an ambulance goes speeding
Through the darkened night.
My heart skips a beat
As I stand and stare
As that mournful sound
Splits the air.
I don't know who for
I don't know where
But it means more bad news
For someone out there.

John E Shepherd

CLOUDS OVER AFRICA

Saddened clouds lie over Africa,
When will the changes come,
Jesus didn't invent apartheid,
Every day a Soweto woman loses a son.

Look at the black children crying,
Under the dark African skies,
There's bloodshed in the township,
Look at the children
With their hands over their eyes.

The newsreels and the papers,
spitting out white men's lies,
Let the children play together,
Let the children have some fun.

Every black man that dies,
Is another black man's son,
No life for them who live under the shadow
of the gun.

J M Wallace

THE STORM

The storm is raging what a night
The moon, and stars are out of sight
Dark clouds like mountains, fill the sky
Leaves, and twigs, come racing by
We walk along the lonely road
No one around, it's much too cold
Our hands, and toes are turning blue.
At last, our home comes into view
Shelter at last from freezing snow
Instead, a welcome from the fire's glow

B Gibson

THE STARGAZER

A black silhouette steps out from the shadows.
Proudly, he strolls along the brick wall.
His head and tail held high.
An emerald glistens, as his eyes catch a shaft of moonlight,
And his coal black fur wafts in the cool crisp night air.
The solitary stranger, looks majestically up into the
                                        deep royal blue night sky.
A diamond sparkling in the distance winks at him,
                                        as if it were keeping some great secret.
The breeze drops to nothing, and he closes his saucer eyes.
He stops and listens . . . to silence.
He sees those, who weep,
Merciful sinners at the feet of ignorance.
His breath mists on the clean coolness.
He listens. He understands. He is the stargazer.

Lisa Thompson (13)

HER SPIRIT HAS FLOWN

I felt the presence of her spirit, although the woman had long gone,
away from what she would have called the tragedy of her youth.
Many days we used to walk together, talk together,
dreaming of an enduring destiny.
I see now the fire is sinking low,
only the embers left to glow.
For a moment I linger and look at the clock with
its ticking finger,
it points beyond midnight, I now realise her spirit has flown.

C M Brackley

I'M OUT OF WORK

The day has dawned, the sun's in the sky
Another long day for me, to get by
I stand by the window, see people go to work
Which I have been accused of trying to shirk
It's no fun being on the dole
It can blow your mind, and destroy your soul
For job after job, you try and you try
Refusal after refusal, you cry and you cry
The tunnel is so long, you can't see the light
I don't think I can get through another long night
With a wife to keep, and children to feed
Doesn't anyone know, it's a job I need
I think of the times I could pay my way
With the present system, poverty's here to stay
I was raised to work hard, and earn my bread
But I'm afraid to now say I wish I were dead
I'm behind with my mortgage, my house needs repairs
And the sorrowing thing is that nobody cares
When you're out of work, you are on your own
The scrapheap you think, is where you've been thrown
You tramp the streets, heart full of hope
And tell yourself, I can cope, I can cope
Then the truth dawns, I'm not by myself
There's millions of others been put on the shelf
It's a terrible thought, when you realise
This industrious nation is nearing its demise
With privatisation here and redundancies there
The workforce of this nation looks on with despair
When will the people in power sit up and take note
It's the workforce of this nation, that casts the vote

William Miller

WHAT IS LIFE REALLY WORTH?

We are born
  onto this earth.
But what is life
  really worth?

What do we do
  in our short time.
Except leave others
  who, for us pine.

Sent to school
  for us to learn.
Creating the dreams
  for which we yearn.

Off to work
  to earn the right.
To pass each day
  without a fight.

Pension time
  with old age.
Very little money
  not even a wage.

Shortly it's time
  to leave this earth.
So what is life
  really worth?

J Muttock

THE PICTURE IN MY MIND . . .

The wind coming off the sea with its persuasion, gently closes my eyes,
I start to paint a picture in my mind, the blue green sea now turns
Into a black mass of leaking filth from a stranded ship, one moment of
carelessness destroys so much, sea birds as black as coal, wings glued
Together, eyes burning, fish and seals float in time with the tide, back
and forth, what must their last moments of life been like?
The picture in my mind turns from green meadows, sweet smelling
flowers, birds and insects, to grey unending roads that take us back to
where we started from, cats' eyes that light the darkness to give the
car its priority, give it space, give it more room to pollute and tear
at our lungs with its poisons, how long can this go on?
The picture in my mind turns to red, not from the sunset but from the
bodies of those butchered in war, friend against friend, take no
prisoners, limbs torn from bodies, men women and child alike, more
madness unable to stop, what is the need . . . why?
The picture in my mind turns from the good brown soil to the starving
people of the world, old and young, men and women, hunger chooses its
victims with care, always the weakest, the poor the unfortunate, hold out
your hand to span the world, you will find plenty to hurt your
eyes, but what you see is not for you, don't ask, don't expect.
The picture in my mind grows darker without colour, without form or
shape, the wind coming off the sea with its persuasion, gently opens my
eyes . . .

Jeff Chick

LOVE

And time stood still.
The world held its breath
as my mind
was held in yours,
held in mine.

Eternity was passing.
Beauty froze in crystals
as my being
was merging in yours,
merging in mine.

Someday maybe
it will be as nothing.
But for now
let it shiver into being
let it gather into kisses
let it pulse into our heartbeats
let it melt into our arms.

Fern Hughes

A MESSAGE TO THE WORLD

The destruction of our planet
Is there for all to see
The smog the grime, the forests decline
For progress of humanity
The pollution of our precious seas
Being rubbed of all its life
All for the sake of the wretched rich
To buy furs and mink for their wives
If only governments could see all this
And let common sense prevail
The wildlife still will roam the plain
And the seas will still have a whale
So stop it now you greedy lot
Before it all gets too late
Or suffer in the future years
When man will have the same fate.

Ronald Elgar

GENERATION GAMES

Hello there! Little teddy,
I haven't seen you for a while;
You've still got mischievous eyes
and a winsome smile.

You were once best friends
with my little boy.
When he was only three
you became his favourite toy.

He took you everywhere
when he was just a tot.
You kept a nightly vigilance
while he slept in his cot.

And then when he was eight
you were banished to a drawer,
He said that he'd grown up
and didn't want you anymore.

Teddy, I must tell you
something you don't know:
He met a girl and fell in love;
they were wed a year ago.

Now he's sent for you
for his brand new baby boy.
You'll be loved again teddy,
as befits a cuddly toy.

K H McGeeney

AUTUMNAL WALK

As I do trudge the silent dawn,
with eyes that see and blood quite warm,
The mist shroud fields a glint of sun
another wondrous day begun.

Gossamer woven on the grass
reminds one of the winter's frost.
Leaves of red some of yellow
gently fall like coloured feather.

Watch the mist roll down the river,
which give a ripple then a quiver.
Down below fish swim silent by,
whilst birds above soar in the sky.
These simple things that God provide
makes one glad to be alive.

I Blaseby

THE YOUTH

A youth setting out on his journey through life
By a wise man was given this piece of advice
When problems beset you, as surely they will
Then look for that rainbow just over the hill

The time's always darkest, at just before dawn
Then follows the sun and a new day is born
Things seldom are really as bad as they seem
And tomorrow, today, will be yesterday's dream

You see on life's journey there's no turning back
And the wisdom of Solomon most of us lack
So each of us must do the best that we can
To achieve the goals set in our own master plan

The youth having heeded the wise man's advice
Took comfort from this as he journeyed through life
And when in his old age he paused to look back
It was clear to him then, it had been the right track

Michael C Eames

FREE IN LIFE

If you just look around you
There's so much that is free
The sky above, the clouds on high
The rivers and the sea
The bluebells in the fields
The smell of new mown hay
The stars up in the sky at night
The sun that gives its ray
The rivers slowly flowing
The salmon going to spawn
The birds so high up in the sky
They start to sing at dawn
The moon that men have walked upon
Is there for us to see
The tide that laps along the beach
Is there for you and me
The waterfalls cascading
Giving out its awesome spray
The trees and flowers come to life
Around the month of May
Just come with me and go outside
There's so much more to see
It doesn't cost a penny
'Cause everything is free

Elizabeth Shaw

DARKER DAYS

Nights draw in, it's dark for eight,
Summer's gone, winter won't wait,
The wind blows the trees to see if they're ready,
For leaves to fall off and make sure that they are steady,
To take all the weather winter will bring
With wind, rain and snow there's no birds left to sing

So make sure you're all comfy, with fire and with light,
Yes! I know when the snow comes it's a real pretty sight,
But - nicer it is to be all of a glow
With fire, light and food
Sat wi' folks that you know.
To sit with a book or knitting to do,
Making plans for next summer
Just to help winter through.

Nora Yeomans

WHY?

I was once a happy confident girl
Ambitious about my forthcoming world.
But it wasn't to be,
No, not for me.
My schooldays were to be snatched away
Without me having any say.

Why did she pick on me?
Was i different, something I couldn't see.
Had I done something wrong?
Sung the wrong note in her life song.
It is one part of my life I will always wish I could change,
Then maybe I wouldn't have been in her firing range.

I kept it a secret for as long as could be
Lying about things I didn't want people to see.
But then it all became too much,
I began to lose all possible touch.
I hid myself away,
Promising I'd say something, some day.

And when I did, she got off scot-free,
And the girl in the corner, that'll always be me.

Katie Ferrier (15)

MY FRIEND, JODIE

On one cold November morn
I opened my back door
A little kitten came to me
It hadn't long been born.

It had no name or place to go
So friendly was its way
I could never be its foe
I wanted it to stay.

I took it in the fire was warm
I gave it milk to drink
Remember it was only dawn
And I, its only link.

It stayed with me and wouldn't go
My friend it wished to be
Its chance of life was very low
If it hadn't come to me.

I named it 'Jodie' as was right
It was surely going to stay
Its colour lovely black and white
It had surely lost its way.

But now it's grown to a lovely cat
The house belongs to her
She fed so well and got quite fat
I'm pleased to hear her purr.

I'm glad our Jodie came to me
It must have been her fate
Kindness we have got to see
Or, it just could be too late.

M Howarth

DEATH OF A TREE (LONDON)

The scream rent the air
The thick soft throat was threaded with rings of life,
Yet how still she lay, no sound of whispering leaves,
Just a thud as she hit the ground.

How long have you stood, how many wild moons have you seen?
How oft has thy golden hair rustled in the night?

The cruel rope around thy neck, the biting knowing saw,
The grinning beast, the flight of life, the ugly stump of death.

I saw you cry, your life force poured out of you,
I cried with you, when they lifted you high, by rope and chain.

The men beasts swept the skin of thee,
You were gone,
No rest for thee like Keats,
Shelley has thy sisters, Cypress tall.

I see thee in the dawn of life;
Your silence casts no shadow now
I cry like a lone bird, calling to thy shattered hull.

The stilled machines move on,
No thrushes will sing in thee, no beetles mate no more,
No drunk will hug thee,
I sob for thee, as you sob as you die,
From bitter foe.

V J M Chadwick

THE GOOD OLD DAYS

I've been sitting here thinking of days of old,
Not as far back as when knights were bold!
But to the days of my youth, and aniseed balls,
Penny vantas bottles, and music halls!

When the 'bobbies' walked the beat in pairs,
while at home we sat on horse-hair chairs!
I remember Pedigree, and Silver-Cross prams,
and the old bone-shaking open front trams!

At Christmas, mum bought peat blocks to burn,
And 'milky' sold milk, straight from the churn,
If 'chesty', goose-grease brought you back to your prime,
And Friday night was laxative time!

Remember the man, selling large blocks of salt,
and your daily dose of cod-liver oil, and malt?
What about sticky-lice, and liquorice sticks?
And 'catties' and 'proddies' never would mix.

Your wellies, in winter, would chaff your bare legs,
and the gypsy will curse you, if you don't buy her pegs!
Steam Sentinel wagons move with a lurch,
and Sunday walks to the old village church.

The old school board, and the 'nitty' nurse,
the noisy clatter of a horse-drawn hearse,
All these things my old mind recalls,
But what I miss most, are those aniseed balls!

J D Southall

FAR

Oh how clever to scorn so tender an invitation,
Wrapped up with love in Basildon Bond.
How bitter the memory of a callous rejection
So hard to reconcile when the moment's long gone.

Fall back, fall further, fall far,
When present and past collide in despair.
Tear up my past - kill my last dream.
Add another scene to an endless nightmare.

Walk away with no vision, walk far.
Scream desperation to the sea and the mist.
Bar an escape from memories of loss;
From hope I once held and lips I once kissed.

Torrin Clark

CUPBOARD LOVE

Come, my beautiful cat
And sit beside me.
While away the time
And do not stray far
From my side.
Your amber eyes watch me
And my every move,
And take in all I do.
You say nothing, yet
Your eyes speak volumes.
And in the love you show
When you purr and rub
Against my legs,
I feed you, and then you
Turn aside and go away.
In your independence
I am forgotten until the
Next meal comes round,
When you remember me once more,
And all will start again.

Dorothy Biggins

THE DANCING LEAVES

The wind is rustling through the trees
And I can feel its cooling breeze
The leaves are dancing
I can see
I wish that I could dance
Like thee

They're dancing stronger now
I fear
They might let go
And trees be bare
The breeze does blow
And the wind does roar
I hope the little leaves
Don't soar

They're dancing dancing
To and fro
They have no choice
Perhaps
They will let go
But no

The leaves are dancing all around
And I can hear
Their rustling sound
The wind dies down
And the leaves do rest
I can tell you
They danced their best

Elizabeth Eragat

THE BUTTERFLY

Flitting from flower to flower,
Delicacy in a rainbow hue.
Intrigued by your fanciful grace,
Watching, whatever you do.

Wings that beat so brightly,
Ethereal, heavenly, light.
Summer personification,
I gaze as you take flight.

Astonished by your beauty,
Perfectly formed, yet so very small.
You glide with effortless grace,
I marvel as you rise and fall

You are a wonder to me,
What elegance you possess.
A small but complex creature,
A miracle, and nothing less.

Lisa Taylor

LOOKING BACK

A child sits all alone,
The pain she hurts all over.
Her eyes they stare into the unknown,
No-one around, no-one to hold her.
The tears they trickle down her face;
She wonders what she's doing in this damn place.
As she remembers those horrible times,
She needs a mum she can call mine.
Instead she cries herself to sleep
A noise she mustn't say a peep.

Suzanne Hughes

WINTER

Winter is coming
Dark days ahead
I hear you say
Nights draw in
People hurry home
Under the winter sky

Winter is a time to rest
Time to take stock
Animals hibernate and people go to night class
Will it be poetry or prose?
Who knows what winter will bring
In this season of harsh blustery days

Winter's discontent will be our gain
Drawing on our strength, to rekindle our faith
Out of the ashes we will create our best ever
Time to continue in life's struggle to win
Each and everyone back into our faith
In this season of savage destruction

Kate Davies

WRONG TIMES

Folk always seem to call on days that I decorate my place
When there's paintpots on the floor and whitewash on my face
It's just my luck they always come to catch me unawares
As bits and bobs and books and things are cascading down my stairs

Old newspapers and letters too, I tend to leave around
But amidst my jumble there I know, where each one can be found
I know I am disorderly but I don't give a damn,
If when folk come they always find me exactly as I am.

My clothing could lie anywhere instead of on the pegs
While shoes I toss across the floor just to save my legs
I hesitate to tackle a job lest I cause a hullabaloo
'Cos every time I start on one, I end up making two.

So if I know you're coming here, I'll organise myself
I'll tidy up that living room and those knick-knacks on my shelf
Always you will be welcome if you're coming round to tea
And if you find things ship-shape then, of course that won't be me.

J W Cash

MACBETH AND I

Macbeth's tomorrow sometimes seems all too much like mine.
My thoughts of sooty doom like his are also foul and fair;
Foul to superficial eyes, but fair to my crazed blinks.
I see through him a life much worse and yet with mine it has its links.

The murd'rer had a leaping aim to which he did succumb.
Both wife and witches urged him on with threats and prophesy.
My perfection is a risk because what if I pale?
Both school and teachers urge me on with force and make me scared to fail.

Macbeth's spouse knew the straining burden she exerted.
She understood the part she played and gave in to her guilt.
My school and teachers claim to know the cross they make me bear.
If this is so then should they not share the fate of the tragic pair?

Macbeth had chosen not to die on the Roman sword,
But I don't have a worthy clash to lose with honoured fame.
I can only snuff the flame and sack my fretting mime.
When freed then I can only hope there is an author behind time.

Mary Chester-Kadwell

THOUGHTS OF A YEAR

January thoughts are cold and dull,
No more Christmas or Hogmanay over which to mull.
February, chill, with falling snow,
Yet the daylight hours begin to grow.
March, winds that sing, promising
the sun filled days of spring.
April, with its many showers,
Gardens bedecked with gilly flowers.
May, when birds get little rest
feeding fledglings in their nest.
June, the grass so green, the rising corn,
days are long, summer is born.
July, scent of honeysuckle in the air,
wild berries gathered, for the strawberry fayre.
August, when butterfly and bee,
flit from flower to flower in endless rivalry.
September, men's backs to bend unto the plough,
for harvest grain is all gathered now.
October, leaves to sunset colours change,
Jack Frost with icy finger through the night doth range.
November, pale sunbeam, brief darkening day,
fallen leaves obstruct the weary travellers way.
December, and the end of the year,
sweet notes of the robins song I hear;
The stain of red upon his breast,
reminds us all that God does not rest,
He will bring the new year to life again,
With sunshine after snow and rain.

Maureen Richardson

THOUGHTS DURING A HANGOVER

Looking at life through rose tinted glasses
Watching as everything in life passes
The numb early morning hangover haze
It's going to be a never-ending day
What was it that was said, what did it all mean
So there it was it was just a dream
But could I be the next James Dean?
The friends I have, the others who've gone
Was it me who drove them away,
With a careless word or a joke gone wrong
Listen to early morning radio songs
Lyrics which say 'sorry' or 'I want you back'
Close your eyes and fade to black
Work takes away the thought of any pain
Inside it's warm and dry while outside it rains
Everyone asking questions, my patience they try
I need more time and money, I deserve a pay rise
Some of the time, hours seem to drag
Pass a little time with a smoke on a fag
Never enough hours just to stop and think
Carefully laid plans have gone to waste
Too many things have been done in haste
Dreams and ambitions shattered by the things I have forgot
Where am I now, getting back to the plot
Like I said I've just forgot.

Steve Cooke

LOVE IN ALL WEATHER

Phone rings, the mellow tone,
date set, pick up at home.
Best dress, excitement pains,
remember brolly in case it rains.

Eyes meet, the fusion starts,
hands touch, stir in the heart.
First kiss, passion smoulders,
but outside it's getting colder.

Second date, must hurry,
doorbell rings, all a flurry.
Open arms, pleased to see,
snow started at half past three.

Snuggle closer, keeping warm,
tongues meet, reason gone.
Sensual bliss, appetite replete,
now the snow has turned to sleet.

True love, wedding bells,
monthlies missed, baby swells.
Event awaited, nerves shattered,
All the rain showers will be scattered.

Baby arrives, the family complete,
bottles made, nappies stacked neat.
More love comes with three together,
Sun shines, but never mind the weather.

Joan Lister

JUST DO IT!

I was the one who said to be careful,
I knew the value of security,
I thought about the rainy days,
I thought my approach showed maturity,
the reckless are clueless!
Living for now doesn't make sense!
You only think you're happy!
Your lives have no substance!

I was wrong,
I admit it,
before your philosophy I bow,
those who look too far into the future,
are only missing out on now,
imagine looking to each new day,
and doing all you can to make it a ball,
now and forever can be good,
and this attitude needn't lead to a fall,
you'll be happier,
live longer,
be more confident,
the love of life will be stronger,

I am converted,
though it's hard to shake off the past,
and I don't exactly live each day,
as though it is my last,
but I'm getting there,
if at times my progress is slow,
I believe it is the way to be,
and I wish I had realised long ago.

Neil Gibson

THE PEDLAR OF SHADOWS

Beyond the furthest mountain where tomorrow meets today,
A pedlar sorts out shadows, softest shadows, blue and grey.

The pedlar chooses carefully the shadows that are right,
And steals away those shadows in the stillness of the night.

The shadows take their colours from the ground on which they lay
From the person that they followed, and the tints that stained the day.

And there among the mountains, in his home beyond the mists,
He sorts them into fragrant piles and marks them off on lists.

He takes the smallest shadows gleaned in the early dawn
And makes them into softest shawls for children yet unborn.

From shadows that are strong and bold, the pedlar forms a sail,
To carry souls to glory when they are weak and frail.

He sews some into saddles for the awesome lordly ones,
And gauntlets for their lordly hands to hold their swords of bronze.

So if you wake one morning, and your shadow is not there
Even though you know you left it lain upon your chair,

You'll know the shadow pedlar has stolen it away
To beyond the furthest mountain where tomorrow meets today.

Dorothy Beaumont

ROOTS OF GOLD

Poetry trickles through my veins
It ripples through my mind,
The hidden treasures of the soul
We sit and think to find.

Poetry vibrates through my bones
As the freedom felt is found,
The roots of gold that glisten
So deep within this ground.

Poetry oozes from my pores
My tears form pools of verse,
Rhymes that form the wings of love
Whose flight gives fright to curse.

Poetry may remove the pain
Of life's indifferent day,
Like a sacred text of whispers
That is teaching us to pray.

Les Lambert

THE END OF LIFE

Broken twisted bodies are strewn around,
The nauseating stench of blood as it runs into the ground,
Pitiful cries from the wounded dying people,
While prayers are directed towards the distant church steeple.

Buildings being set alight as shops are being looted,
Fast cars being driven at the innocent women and children,
The police have long gone, they were the very first to die,
Political answer was to drop bombs from high in the sky.

Bloodied fist and boot create this new revolution,
Women are raped as children watch in fascination,
Even the strongest can fall from bullets and sharp steel,
Death can be kind, a release from the pain you feel.

In amidst this nightmare, one man still stands proudly,
Surveying this scene and listening to frightened screams,
Yet he is sorrowful, for this is of his creation,
This hell upon earth, upon which we were imprisoned.

Eventually, as the final screaming abates and flames cease to flicker,
The one we call messiah has to evaluate to cost,
The toll will be high, but he knows the good people chosen, will pay the
price
For a new life is nigh. As our saviour walks away . . .

S L Smith

FALSE HOPE

You've let me down once again
you only added to my pain
I don't know how long I can go on
For what you do to us is so very wrong
you send me into turmoil you see
with all the things that you've said to me
you gave me hope then you took it away
and you made me face another day
My life is so lonely and empty now
I try to get through it somehow
I pray for you every day and night
as I struggle along in my plight
My heart is broken in two
and all I can think of is you
you stay away each and every day
but that just fills me with dismay
I think of you in all that I do
Oh how I wish I didn't love you
my feelings for you I just can't hide
like a wave upon a tide
I'm waiting for you to come in
and thinking of all that might have been
It hurts me so much not to be part of you
and share the things we used to do.

Elizabeth Leach

INNA CITY BLUES

I see your streets once
  paved with gold
   - now battered and worn

I see your people once
  filled with hope
   - now sunk in despair

I see your children once
  happy smiling faces
   - now they dream no more

Oh England! Oh England!
Where is your hope
       and glory now?

Prince Nugent

FORLORN

I've listened to your tale of woe,
A sorry tale, as tales will go,
I've listened to your aches and pains,
It always pours, it never rains.

No silver in a cloud for you,
The sky is grey, it's never blue
I hear you talk, of your bad luck,
Instead of money, you've got muck

No pot of gold, at rainbow's end,
And how you've just, lost your last friend,
Down hard luck's road, you say you're walking,
All alone, nobody talking.

You pour it out to me each day
Because, I cannot get away
For I see you, every morning,
Through the mirror, always moaning.

You really are a jinx, a jonah,
Every day, another trauma.
You wonder why, you're on your own,
I wish you could go, and leave me alone.

George Parr

FALSE ARREST

Hear me officer, it was not I
Who was making all that din
Amongst the flower beds and shrubs

But a smiling individual
Who came gliding across my path
He was laughing and singing

Could it be that it was he
All draped in red robes
With a long white flowing beard

He was in such haste
He declined to stop and pass the night away
His description fits what you have said

A large boisterous looking fellow, you say,
Making all kinds of noise, I'm sure that it was he
What makes me sure, was the vehicle he rode

A long sleigh filled with parcels galore,
Six fine young reindeer tugging at the reins,
Bells adorned their heads, it was the bells you heard pealing

That was the din you arrested me for
Pray let me be, stand back I say
You have no need of me

Look up yonder to the sky
There he goes trailing a blaze of stars
It is he, *Santa Claus.*

Marilyn Boil

GETTING IN THE SWIM OF THINGS

Gettin' in the swim of things
That's what I try to do
So I joined the local night class
Just for a week or two
With next door neighbour Rene
We trotted off to see
What we could do in water
That came above the knee

With nervous apprehension
We stood beside the pool
Observed a young instructress sitting on a stool
She took our name and number
And with a friendly smile
Said just go in the water, and play about a while
We gingerly crept down the steps, looking rather pale
Our knuckles going white, with clutching at the rail

The water it was 4'6" and we only 5'2"
So we didn't reckon much to it, and started going blue
We felt our lungs were bursting
And couldn't get our breath
In fact if we were truthful, it frightened us to death

But now we've been a time or two
Our attitude's more calm
We have a blown up rubber band, encircling either arm
We bob about and do our best
And perhaps one night you'll find
Me and my friend Rene
Swimming with the rest
'Cause that friendly young instructress
Is one of the very best.

J Atkin

AUTOMATION

Born with blue eyes, lovely blonde hair
Happy smiling, folks would stare
Fun and games down by the sea
Then picnics in the wild country
Schooldays so happy, cycling through
Camping, football, baseball too
Joined the Cubs became a Scout
Did odd jobs to help folks out
A choir boy in red and white
Then fireworks on Guy Fawkes Night
Christmas with so many toys
Things that amused most little boys
Left school with 'A's' and then Degrees
The world's his oyster was not to be
Alas the crunch he tried in vain
To find a job all with no gain
The usual sorry, sorry, no, no, no
That same reply nowhere to go
He flipped and sported tatty jeans
Pale black shirts, all ripped, unclean
Now so uncouth and language sour
This is not our son this hideous shower
Living rough in squats and fields
With others in remorse
High on drugs wasting away
A corpse they'll be soon any day
Yet here were brains and hands for work
Automation took over, that damn berk!

Laura O'Halloran

FOR NICHOLA

Sunday arrives, it's the twelfth of November,
Nichola is here - is that a temper?
Jumpy; on edge; can't sit still for a second,
Frightened? Up tight? Or has somebody beckoned?
Who was it - *what* was it; if anything at all,
That promised and urged her to answer that call?

No money, no assets, no recompense,
To spend on this nonsense that doesn't make sense.
Can't borrow, such sorrow, just have to steal,
Don't matter, *it* leads me; don't care how I feel.
I've *got* it, it's good and it's over for now,
I won't take it tomorrow - that's my promise and vow.

Tomorrow is here and the feeling is near,
I need it - I want it - it's gonna be dear.
I'll get it; I'll have it no matter the cost,
Take a risk here or there, there's nought to be lost,
But this hole, where my soul was my being; my whole,
Is empty and vacant and no use at all.

I shan't dwell on family and loves of my life,
or sadness and hates and insurmountable strife.
It's the path that I chose; the path of my fate,
It won't lead me to heaven, it just goes to hell's gate.
But I know there's a chance, for I know of God's love,
It was sent by my granddad from heaven above,
If I let him, he'll lead me and love me forever,
He'll hold me and help me and be here, as ever.

S J Alexander

LAUREN

Lauren you lie there so peaceful, with a mint coloured blanket covering your small body, you're so beautiful, with that face of an angel and eyes that will melt ice. You are the youngest of four, and the cheekiest, but what would we do without you, your three sisters smother you like three little mothers. I am so proud, so happy, my heart is filled with love that could burst into springtime. You were not planned but I thank God you are here, I hear you say, 'I spy with my little eye something beginning with, my friends.' Out the mouth of our baby, our little girl so sweet so comforting, so pure! You changed our whole life darling, you made us become a family. I enjoy life now, more than I could have ever. You made me sit down and think, you made me make the right choice. I look at you and wonder what your mind thinks about, a mind of innocence. Your hair looks like threads of silk and Lauren your cheeks become rose red, we should have called you Snow White. And who would have thought that a two-year old little girl could have brought all this.

Julie Bolam

MOTHER

More than all the gold in the world
Or pearls from the deepest seas
These together don't mean -
    As much as you mean to me
Heaven's angels up above can -
    Never take your place
Even though you're far away -
    I can still see your loving face
Remember, dear mother my thoughts -
    Are there and that I really care

Gavin Dodds

YOUNG TOM

The night air beckons, mysterious and cool
As darkness seduces and shadows summon.
Instinctively, young Tom responds
To the enigmatic bidding of the midnight call.

A magnificent creature with a large head
And sharp green eyes that pierce the gloom.
Fine back arches and hackles rise
As senses function on red alert.

And he prowls and skulks and slinks unseen
In the swirling shadows and veiled mists;
Sneaking his way among hidden places,
Stalking his prey with lethal intent.

Claws unsheathed and programmed to kill!
A ruthless aggressor with fire in his blood.
He's a gangster cat and utterly fearless,
Scrapping, even now, in some hellish abyss.

With ears torn and bleeding flanks,
Neck scratched and teeth bared,
Yet, battle-scarred, he emerges the victor,
Limping home as cold dawn breaks.

It's dull, austere and sterile now
Until a pale yellow disc begins to glow,
But young Tom's unmoved, curled fast asleep,
Impervious to the day's first light.

Linda Bitvus

A NOVEMBER WALK

While walking through the woods of brown
On a late November day
Upon my face a snowflake fell
Settling, as if to say
'Has wintertime arrived at last,
Can I bring my kindred down?'
Not waiting for an answer
The flakes my head did crown
They fell in thousands from the sky
Twisting and dancing gay
They filled me with such sweet delight
As I strolled on my way
A carpet soon appeared in white
It was a sight indeed
With just my footsteps through the wood
As the cool fresh air I breathed
But all too soon the sun came out
Melting my carpet white
My snowflakes soon a pool of mud
No longer a heavenly sight

Muriel Roe

FORECASTING RAIN

The old dog with back legs
As battered as the wind is strong, in March,
Comes in, lies down, looks up.
'The general synopsis' is being read
To a steaming white enamel cup, behind which
Is a purple faced fisherman.

The old man lets Shannon's variable pass,
And the well trained mouth of Oxford's son
Is about to come down upon Fairisle, when,
Cap raised, beard trawling the dregs of the tea,
The fisherman flicks the noise off, like a tic
Or a flea, and summons the dog to his side.

She is prodded and ruffled a while,
And the fisherman finds that indeed
There are east north east gales and
With the thunder the rain has come -
Why else would the old girl be in?
And he sits fast in the storm, wondering
What knowledge the mainland is teaching the young.

M Remblance

EYES OF MINE

Silent tears roll from my eyes
Mine is not to reason why
Gently down my cheeks they flow
Is it of sorrow or of woe?

Should I begin to understand why?
These big brown eyes of mine do cry
Could it be deep within my heart?
All this pain alas did start.

On and on they pour and pour
What on earth can this be for?
Face and hair all is wet
Why would I be so upset?

A voice rises way inside.
Stop it now, wipe those eyes.
What you feel you can't disguise
Tears that fall tell no lies.

Anita Craig

AT HAMPTON COURT

At Hampton Court, on a mellow August day,
In fragrant beds, lush blooms did softly sway,
Stroked by the kiss of nature's gentlest breeze.
Capricious butterflies and plump, contented bees
Danced with the ghosts of carefree young princesses,
In quaint plumed hats, and silk embroidered dresses.

By mighty Thames, the haughty royal swans bickered,
As shimmering fish beneath the surface flickered,
Whilst merry laughter floated on sweet haze;
Disembodied voices perplexed within the maze,
And sparkling fountains quiveringly applauded
The handsome palace they courteously lauded.

In the Great Hall's splendour, crowned by beams decorous,
Pert-faced eavesdroppers piously watched o'er us,
Silent, as they strained enchanted ears
To witness shameful falsehoods through the years,
And proud stags' heads stared down with glassy eyes,
In mourning for their species' sad demise.

To Wolsey's closet, time-worn stairs ascended.
An icy grip of hopelessness impended.
The gallery, sublime with masters rare,
Became consumed within a fog of black despair,
As unseen spirits contritely implored:
Eternal rest
        Grant unto them, O Lord.

Margaret Turner

DURHAM (DUNHOLME)

The monks travelled for many a year
Carried the saints, so precious, with care.
They rested awhile, in a place called Dunholme
From there, they would no longer have to roam.
It was on a high bluff, above the Wear
That snakes from high hills to ocean clear.
This would be, the saints' last home
There, they built a church, of wood and stone.
A church that would stand for eternity
A cathedral, for a saintly three.
Where Oswald, Cuthbert and Bede could rest
In the Northumbria, they all loved best.
Where chevronned columns rise on high
Supporting Norman arches in the sky.
Where memorials hewn from local coal
Are testaments, to the brave miner's soul.
And gargoyle knocker on the door
Once provided sanctuary from the law.
Where stained glass windows still tell
Of northern saints who once did dwell
In this green and pleasant land
Bound by high hills and salt sea sands.
Where the great tower rises high
To provide a lantern, to light the sky.
To proclaim, to all around
That this is holy and sacred ground.
Where heavenly choirs still will sing,
In praise and glory to Christ the King!

K Porritt

PEEVISH WOMEN

Be not peevish, spiteful, sly;
Lest the years may pass you by,
And leave you with your lips of ice
That no man ever dare entice.

One day you may want to smile,
But find your lips to stiff awhile;
Only a sigh escapes - 'Too late!
I'll never get another date.'

'Tis to the good to wear this mask,
All against nature? You may ask!
To think you're saddled with this now,
That nature did not you endow.

So wipe away this horrid smirk,
Let pleasantry shine through the murk,
'Real beauty cometh from within,'
Too late, you ponder, to begin?

But try you must to shed this lust,
Before you rot away to dust,
So gaze some more at your reflection,
See you now your imperfection.

"Twill be no use' I hear you say,
'But I'll continue to mend my way,
And look a little way beyond,
This beauty I've so greatly wronged.'

You'll still meet nature face to face,
But look around and act with grace,
'Oh cursed mask begone' you say,
'Stay not with me another day.

I do not want your sneery gaze,
You make all feel in the devil's maze,'
Take heed! If not, you've made your bed,
Thus to abide with bowing head.

James Coneys

LONELY AND OLD

When the back door closes
And she locks her bolts and chain
She sits in her chair with the cat on her knee
And wonders if it will rain

How will she pay the gas bill
Did she put all the shopping away
Did she hide her purse in the usual place
Is that programme she likes on today

Could this be your mother
Could she be lonely and sad
Do you think of yourself every day of your life
Or are you not quite that bad

When will you try to see her
Will it be too late
Or will you go tomorrow
Will she hear the click on the gate

You know she'll be so happy
Her face will light up with joy
Forget your selfish feelings
You are her favourite boy

All right, so you are sixty
With important things to do
But remember that will be you one day
And will I think the same about you

Karen Brown

WHY ARE YOU BACK?

When I saw you after all those years, you made the memories come flooding back, oh what happy days. You didn't even see me, you don't even know you've turned my life upside down.

I bet you wouldn't even recognise me now, I've changed so much. I'm engaged now, he's a really nice man, who would do anything for me and until you came back, I thought I loved with all my heart. Now after seeing you again, I wonder?

Why did my heart feel empty, when I saw her next to you, laughing cuddling . . . she'll be good for you, but not like I was. We had a past, we helped each other through the rough times and I feel I should be in her place, laughing, cuddling, kissing . . .
When my fiance, tells me he loves me, I know he really means it but, all I can think about is you. You used to say that to me, I feel mean, disloyal, but I can't help it.

Why am I even thinking like this? You left me, left me all those years ago, by myself; I had to pick up the pieces that you had left behind and when I finally got myself back on my feet again, and I thought over you, I met someone, someone really special to me, who loves and respects me for who I am, not what I look like.

We were so long ago and now I'm living in the present, I'm not a little kid anymore, I have plans, ambitions, I've got opinions and I can express them, unlike I could when I was with you.

When we were together I changed, you said for the better I admit it, I did at the time but now I know I was living to please you, anything you wanted, I got for you, I did everything for you, you were my life. With my new boyfriend I've got my own life, he's got his own life, but together we are inseparable.

I'm just telling you so you know how I feel, I love him. I don't know what I felt for you, but it was certainly not love.

We were together in the past and that is where we'll stay *forever*.

Sandra Marie Turner

ROWTH 'O RHYMES WITH RODENTS

I have lived with laughter daily and I'm now an OAP.
I think laughter's prophylactic and very good for me
I used to be a teacher and I would often tell
My pupils that it was my *smiles* that kept me well,

Then I'd tell them some wee crackers just to wake them up,
And the smiles would slowly broaden as I asked them to make them up
'Can you tell me the difference . . .' is one I used to tell.
I also told them limericks and 'knock knock' jokes as well,

Then I'd joke about the Bible and quote the bluest bits I knew,
As well as ridicule every effete 'God Creator' view,
I would tell them it is *nonsense,* what is seen in Genesis,
I would also say of virgin birth, 'What *utter lies* this is.'

All these laughs I was creating were education at its best
For thought is spurred by *doubt* is a *first rule* that I attest
All true knowledge comes from *doubting* the *lies* that *preachers* tell
This is why my kind of teaching made my pupils all do well.

I did not only teach obedience, I taught criticism and doubt,
With laughter as a weapon to keep us well and stout,
But I am not a cynic, let me make this very clear,
If I had been a pessimist I would not be rhyming here,

I reject all mythic stories made up by lying folk.
Dirty rats like *lying churchmen* are a most unfunny joke
I abhor all talk of praying and the international ring
Who say God and King and Prom songs are what we should sing.

I think a world of armied nations is *top recipe* for *strife,*
And I blame *part-world presidents* for making this our *life!*
We should make the World *one nation,* as the *correct recipe,*
To combine all social movements in *global democracy.*

Edward Graham Macfarlane

NOSTALGIA

As I grow old - looking back
Into the past on bygone days
Everything changes it does not last

Time when doors were always open
No TV no PVC
People were poor - it did not matter
As long as we had - a bit of a natter

The dolly tub's in the back yard
Also greasy fat lard
Washing hanging on the line
(I guess they were mine)

Pleasures and pursuits I fear
Are different now it seems
Money is the root of all evil
Drugs and rackets to I hear
Working men on low pay
Murder's unheard of the way it is today

Days and months vanish into the flame of life's ember
Memories still remain untarnished
For those who do remember.

V A Tunstall

BUSINESS AND MONEY

Over the land under the sea, from the heavens
to a world of beauty and wonder.
How long will it last, with man's rape
and pillaging of the land and sea,
once so great but now so pathetic.

The Amazon once a great river now,
stands alone in once a great jungle.
But now so pathetic as the men
who destroyed her all for the sake
of business and money.

Look at the seal pups watch them
play, and snuggle up to their mothers.
Then watch them die, screaming
like a hundred lost souls, in a sad
plea for mercy to the pathetic
monsters called man, all for the
sake of business and money.

David H Graham

TIME

What was there before time,
Just the pure and sublime.
Did the Creator stand alone,
Is mankind a Godly clone.

It must have taken more than a week,
No more stories, it's the truth we seek.
Mankind was made pure of heart,
The innocence of a child at the start.

The Earth was a garden fair,
Mankind gave it wear and tear.
The Serpent was a part of the plan,
He represented the darker side of man.

Mankind should choose good over ill,
With higher aspirations his senses fill.

Estelle

FREEDOM

Freedom? How do we view this word today?
Most trapped in materialism, simplicity gone astray,
In years gone by, people seemed more content
Yes there were troubles, but not to the extent . . .

Of the present situations, that cause so much stress
Living on adrenaline, not being able to rest,
Instead of happiness, there has become too much sorrow
With many frightened to think, about tomorrow.

People on drugs, others on drink
Hoping their problems will somehow sink,
Into oblivion, and put themselves right
That's *not* how it works, we each have to fight!

Fight for our own freedom, only then will we see
A world at peace, and its people free,
But nobody listens, until it's too late
This is the reason, for so much hate.

Always wanting the best of things
Keeping up with the Jones', but what does it bring?
An elaborate house - a brand new car?
But freedom? Not on *any* credit card!

Sam Williams

LIFE'S PROBLEMS

We live in times as we all know,
When problems by the score,
Confront us, and we wonder what
For us there is in store.

Such problems as inflation
Economy as well,
Of strikes and unemployment
That in our land now dwell.

Of course these problems mentioned,
They are but just a few.
The question now arises,
Just what are we to do?

To find the cause must surely be,
What we must dwell upon,
And when the cause at last we find,
The answer will follow on.

D J Dodd

DESERT DEPRESSION

Living in a timeless void,
This barren landscape of a life,
With no welcoming oasis,
No clear horizons,
Merely mirages of a vibrant future,
Raising expectations,
Only to be dashed in dark
Craters of despair,
And swept away in a
Swirling storm of delusion,
No caravan of consolation,
No pyramid of achievement,
In endless years of doubt,
All hopes obscured by
Shimmering, airborne heat waves,
Mastered only by desert ships,
Cast adrift in this god-forsaken
Moonscaped sea of sand.

Harry Cawood

I WONDER WHO THIS PERSON IS?

Who is this person who
You think of so much
Always there for you to touch
With open arms stretched out for you
When you are feeling down and blue

When you're in trouble and need a friend
She is there no matter when
She brings you up from very small
Through years of patience with us all

Whatever you may say or do
She will always be there for you
Each day and month throughout the years
You should always let her hear
How very much you love her so
Because if she wasn't there
I just don't know

Is this very special person you?
'Yes', I guess you know it's true
I thank you for all you've done
Because without you
There would be no 'Mum'

Mary Butler

WAR

War - domination - death, so much fear
Silence - then the bomb we hear
Run to shelters and under beds
Crouching down to cover heads.

The men went off they waved goodbye,
women and children stand and cry
but off they went to fight a war
       A future - 'never like before'.

The siren sounds, a child screams
The only peace within their dreams.
I only hope one day we'll be
At peace with those that shoot at me.

Many were injured many have died
Everyone was asking why?
They gave their lives to set us free
To make us proud of our country.

J A Stewart

SLAINTE

I don't want to see your face shadowing.
I've seen you travel this road before.
Why do the same mistakes seem so tempting?
I pray you can take no more.

But no, still the hateful juice flows
down your widening, gaping throat.
My anger's as red as your nose
as I watch the puke dry on your coat.

If I was your woman, friends would say bland nothings
to me, and hard nothings to you.
But I'm only your friend, stood watching
the bilious-making water drowning you.

When you hit the floor for the third time
the landlord counts you out.
At last you suss it out . . .
stay down and you don't get hit.

Carrying you crookedly home, sack of potatoes,
to an unmade bed, to an unaired room.
We retch in unison, making the floor glow,
hoping stupored sleep will come soon.

Martin Byrne

MORTAL NEWS

Every last bone in her chilled body shook violently
His words were spoken firmly yet slow
A crowd of faces watched with surges of love and honour
For someone they didn't even know.
Hearts fast beating behind ribs fit to burst.
Staring, all staring - poised in a pregnant age.
The glass which took a thousand years to fall;
Now lay shattered on the floor,
In a million sharp pieces, memories;
The crisp crystal tears of her now seemingly pointless life
He sighed. A long atmosphere crumbling sigh.
His job was done. She had been told.
Now the crowd ran to her aid
Yet it all made no sense.
Half an hour ago her unborn child was alive.

Grainne McMenamin

TRAPPED

Confined in a space,
Locked in a room,
held in time to doom.
Nowhere to go to,
nothing to do!
Without help or understanding.
What life to be trapped.
Alone with no air to breathe
Locked in time and space
What a relief to be
      Trapped.

J M Stones

MY FRIEND

The last rose of summer stood straight and tall.
Its bud tightly closed against the cold.
From my window I watched it slowly uncurl
Its delicate petals the texture of pearls.

This bush was always a favourite with me.
I admired its tenacious attempts to be free.
Neither cold wind or rain stopped its progress in time.
Each morning I looked for the opening sign!

Ah! Yes! There it was, day two showed a break
In the calyx green sheath. The flower was awake!
It twisted and turned throughout the long day.
The first pink petal had come to stay.

The way was now clear for others to follow.
What would I see from my window tomorrow?
The darkness hid my friend from sight,
So I pulled the curtains and wished her, 'Goodnight!'

The following morning was clear and bright.
I flung back the curtains to let in the light.
My rose was now free from her sepal's protection
And stood firm like a candle in all her perfection.

Two weeks of joy were ours each day
As we smiled at each other and I begged her to stay.
But time is relentless and knocks us about.
My dear rose did suffer great loss there's no doubt.

At the end of three weeks there was one petal left.
It was stronger and fairer than all the rest.
With sadness I watched as she tugged herself free
And I knew in my heart she'd waved 'Goodbye' to me.

D M Chatwin

THE GARDENS OF MY PAST

Walking through the gardens of my past
Hearing voices of old friends
That rose bud would have been kicked out of autumn
If I were younger.

Following the paths. I can't remember doing that
The times I ran across the grass
For the danger of a do or die dare
The longing for these days again
Growing more as the memories remain.

The maze of paths and passages
Between the trees and beneath the hedges
Would no more accommodate my size
I see the ghost of my self once more
Ducking and diving through this land.

These gardens hold a lot for me
But now I have learnt a different song
To run and kick and shout and scream
I have grown old and these are wrong.

This was a land where the old didn't live
This was a land where happiness thrived
Where the people were happy
And the grown-ups didn't mind.

But as I say I have climbed this fence
And will never be able to return again
In the garden of futility I will remain
But visit the ghost of where I have been
And to see the thing that I have seen.

I have tried and tried to change this place
To remove its unhappy frowning face
But to no avail I've tried my last
It's true what they say
The future's to come but the past has passed.

Norman Watt

THE TRAMP

Old woman once beautiful
Long ago in her youth
Her weather-beaten face
Tells her story with truth
Of hardships and struggles
She's had by the way
And many's the time
She went without pay
But her eyes they are laughing
A big toothless grin
As she lies there just rocking
With a bottle of gin
Her clothes are all dirty
All tattered and torn
Who am I to despise her
Her lifestyle to mourn
Would I have coped
If I'd had the same life
Five children, no husband
A lifetime of strife
At least now she's happy
Her sorrows are drowned
She's tried everything else
This is the best she has found

Carol Graham

THE LONG LONG ROAD

Down on his luck, he stands in a doorway
Tries to remember some 'old' memory
Clutching his comfort, sips from the bottle
Remembering days that were 'kinder' to 'He'

Only the warmth that he finds in a bottle
He once may have found in the arms of someone
The lips that find solace around some old bottle
Are they the lips of a mother's lost son?

Does he have family or friends who are wondering
What he is doing and where has he gone?
Just one more sip from his 'best friend' the bottle
For family and friends now, he finds he has none.

Just as he's finding the warmth that he craves for
That now soothes the pain and the memories long gone
He takes one more sip of his 'mind blowing' nectar
And hears a voice say 'Would you kindly move on.'

'Would you kindly move on,' and so he does,
Grasping the friend he knows he can trust
Taking a lifetime of unspoken memories
He'll kindly move on, for he knows that he must

He closes his mind to his dreams and his follies
Holds tightly his friend, who will ease all his woes
Once again he starts walking the long lonely highway
It's a very long road when you've no place to go

No place to go to and no one to go with
No one to soften life's blows
Just one more sip from his old friend the bottle
Then down life's weary highway he silently goes.

Annette Patricia Williamson

POLTERGEIST

When the daylight fades and the night's ahead
I listen for the sound of a ghostly tread
I know who's waiting at the bottom of the bed
It's my friendly poltergeist

If there's anything missing - if something should fall
Inextricably suddenly from the kitchen wall
If there just isn't anybody there at all
That's my friendly poltergeist

I'm used to being woken by an eerie sound
While clinging to the bedclothes and floating off the ground
But I'd rather it was you I had my arms around
Oh! How I hate the poltergeist!

When I lie awake and that's a general rule
He'll try to cheer me up by acting the fool
He'll bring along for company his favourite ghoul
Such a friendly poltergeist!

Whenever there's a knocking on the bedroom door
It sends shivers down my spine because I'm never quite sure
That it isn't really you coming back once more
And not a noisy poltergeist

Won't you get the poltergeist away from me please?
Just say you'll come and live with me and set my mind at ease
If we can show him what it is about the birds and bees
. . . Maybe he'll just give up the ghost.

Charles Harry Butler

A SEASIDE RESORT IN WINTER

Once-crowded streets, beach, parking lots
Stand stark and bare.
Forsaken, now that visitors have gone.
Gone too the summer's, searing sun,
For winter's icy hand envelops this deserted place.

How silent is your beach,
At last your own -
The unspoiled playground of the native gulls.
How unattractive are your waters,
Cold and drear -
No screaming children play in uninviting sea.
Only vague outlines of cargo ships can now be seen
Plying their trade to where there still is life.
Silently, lest they should break funereal silence.

The sun still graces you,
But now, his watery rays
Give little comfort to your wintry state.

The pier, like some gigantic finger
Points to warmer climes.
No sound emerges from its trellised frame
Save raucous calls from self-same gulls
Wheeling their flight 'cross leaden sky.

But yet, 'ere long, will once again appear
New life.
Like flower, emerging from its winter's home
Heralding the spring -
The visitor will reappear, like phoenix rising from his winter ashes.
Refreshed -
Rejuvenated -
To quench again his insatiable, summer thirst.

John R Greene

LOVE'S SPIRIT

You're like a ghost in my room
        preying on my mind.
I can sense your touch
        smell your presence,
           you chill the air.

The moon's light illuminates my walls
As it stares at me through my window.
My curtains flap about wildly like two
Sails of the Marie Celeste.
My pulse races, why do you come
Back to haunt me, love's spirit?

Mark Triance

A PEACEFUL TIME

I walked along the forest trail
Admiring the flowers that looked quite frail.
Breathing in the clean fresh air
Wandering on without a care
I came upon a wishing well
I wonder how many secrets it could tell.
Looking at water crystal clear
The faint whispering of trees in my ear
A place so peaceful and tranquil
I lazed there to take my fill
A cuckoo called from time to time
Just to remind me it was not all mine
I stayed and meditated there
Wandering in my dream I know not where
Coming back to reality once more
Deciding it's the prettiest place I've seen for sure
I took my leave walking on
Promising I'd be back before too long

K L Wellington

THE PEACE OF NATURE

I love to be in a garden,
Be it summer, winter or spring,
The smells, the sounds,
And changing colours all year round
Make me feel as though I own the earth.

To feel the soil run through my fingers,
As I plant a bulb, shrub, or tree,
Then the wait for a leaf or flower to appear,
Are moments of joy to me.

As one clears the waste from a garden,
So too one can clear the mind,
Of all the turmoils and worries,
That life plants there -
Sort them out and put them behind.

So, go into a garden,
Look at the small world there,
Full of beauty and life, not trouble and strife,
You will find pleasure you will want to share.

Ann Willow Packwood

THE WAY (SEARCHING ENDS)

Restless hearts never find a place
They keep on running through empty space
Floating by like a cotton cloud
Like a spirit standing tall and proud

Take a ride on a wishing train
Get somewhere in the midnight rain
Stop a while you can't hear no sound
Only shadows walking on the ground

Searching winds carry words unheard
Moving faster than the swiftest bird
Golden dreams carry far and wide
Then gone like waves on the evening tide

Like a memory that slowly fades
Like an old book turning page by page
The darkened cover that feels well worn
Waiting for a time to be newly born

D J Cox

YOU LAUGHED AT MY TEARS

It's years since I left there
Yet I still call it home,
It doesn't seem much easier, it hurts inside.
You gave no chance to make up,
Made the rules to break up.
The least thing that was hurting was my pride

You laughed at my tears - and doubled the hurt.

You told me to leave there,
To pack my bags and go.
You really didn't give me any choice.
I waited each evening for you to come on home
Knowing that you'd been with someone else.

You laughed at my tears - and doubled the hurt.

I'm stronger now by far dear,
Tears no longer fall,
I'm safe within the fortress I've become.
I'm still saddened by the way things are
and what they might have been
and memories of the place I still call home.

D N Gibson

STAY

Another night, another day
yet still you seem so far away,
I've tried so long to make things right,
in this dark tunnel there is no light.

A little murmur you did make,
though you were drastically underweight,
you ventured early into this world,
and into my tunnel I was hurled.

Tubes and monitors all around you,
the sight of which would really astound you,
I sit in silence next to your cot,
thinking of things, I'd have sooner forgot.

Visions and feelings, that just make me cry,
please little darling, hang on there, don't die.
I'm nearing my forties, too old to give birth?
But I need now to tell you, how much you are worth.

If you keep on fighting
and manage to pull through
I promise you darling
I'll always love you

Put light in my tunnel
and love in my heart
then you and me baby
we will never part.

Lorraine Tellis

BONFIRE NIGHT

The scene is just right, the bonfire's alight
the night is as dark as a pit,
the flames are quite small as they dance on the wall
the bonfire is only just lit.

The night is so cold, the flame's getting hold
I think they're beginning to spread
they're jumping quite high to reach to the sky
they're already glowing bright red.

The flames now are hot, they've reached to the top
the bonfire is roaring away,
it lights up the houses, the trees and the fields
and makes it as bright as the day.

We've got to stand back from the roar and the crack
as the bonfire really gets hold
the flames are all dancing and prancing about
in yellow and orange and gold.

The flames getting lower, it's burning much slower
most of the wood is all done,
the chairs and the timbers, the wheels and the tyres
the papers and boxes all gone.

We'll have to get closer, we're feeling much colder
the flames are all dying at last
our beautiful bonfire so sadly has gone,
the flames have reduced it to ash.

C Ormrod

ABSTRACT SERVITUDE

A palette of colour haunts my dreams,
symbolic of my abstract ambience.
Perspective renaissance of my childhood
conscious within harrowing brushstrokes.
Still-life portrait projecting waterbased screaming,
my aspirations closed within a skeletal frame.

Representation depicting silhouette nightmares
in an unstable world of eternal consistency.
Breathtaking detail of agonised expressions
evoked inside a mural of my existence.
Imprisoned on canvas only thoughts for company,
realising the concept of perpetual purgatory.

A collage of emotions spill forth and wash over me
as I gaze up through ambiguous eyes.
The tearful clown dips his brush in the water,
cleansing his past, washing away his future.
Unwieldy impressionism picture-framed
of a still-life, or just a life that is still?

Mark Cope

MY DREAM

Upon a wayside hill lie the small unfolded flowers.
There where people would hunt their kill,
I leisurely sit for hours.
The views across the plain,
the patches of mist, then rain,
the farmers sowing seeds,
their wives plucking the weeds.
I dream of waving seas.
I dream of a cool wet breeze,
On deck I stand waiting for the land.
Ah! There it lies, but it's a fool's paradise.

J Vaughan

CLOSED MINDS

Look at me
and see that I am real.
Look through your hatred and learn I too -
love, laugh and cry,
and like you I have blood flowing
So why stop it with your narrow mind?

Look at me
and see how similar we are.
Look through your anger and learn I am -
no more, no less, no different,
and like you I have a culture
So why stop it with your narrow mind?

Look at me
and see that I am human.
Look through your prejudice and learn I have -
a future, a life, and hopes
and like you I have rights too
So why stop it with your narrow mind?

Look at me
and see war is not the answer
War does not resolve -
only love, only compassion, only understanding
All these can break the barriers and melt stone hearts
So why stop them with your narrow mind?

Janice M Shaw

ANOTHER NEW FIRST

All of a sudden the time was here
I had managed to forget
Put it out of my mind, forget my fear
I was ready, I thought I was set.

It's not till the day comes
That you realise you're not
That you remember other mums
Have survived this same lot.

For weeks we have been preparing
Explaining everything would be new
The clothes she would be wearing
That all her friends would be worrying too.

So today will see her start secondary school
With new uniform, new bag and a few pence,
Time to let go, she's under new rule
She's already sporting a new found confidence,

So today has been my longest day
Watching the clock, waiting for 3.30 to come
Is she enjoying it? It's so important the first day
Here she comes now, 'Well?' I say
And to my delight she replied 'It's brill, mum'.

Christine Saunders

PEACE AT WAR

Missiles fly from sky to ground,
As rain destroying sound on sound,
Bedraggled soldiers kneel to preach,
Missiles fly but never reach.

The battle's won for neither side,
Soul for soul, no need for pride,
Killing kin as they've been taught,
The battle's won, the motive bought.

Silence falls across the plain,
As fighting stops to ease the pain,
Peace at last for those who bled,
Silence falls as all are dead.

John Clarke

'96

For every thought I think it's suicide,
I have it then it dies.
To copy would be genocide,
and all my songs just lies.
So I write them down on paper,
and chain them to the page.
Another jaunt another caper,
another actor on my stage.
Misery's only the absence,
of joy beyond compare.
Replenishment a seance,
fuelled my coldest stares.
The answer to the hatred,
can be found in every hue,
integration is as fated,
yet the others miss the clue.

Tommy Carr

LET LOOSE THE TIES

Let loose the ties and give your children freedom
The new world pioneers, let them stretch and seek out new horizons
Give them no guilt

Allow the young their will, their innovation
Nurture their ideas encourage their expression
Choose love, support, as your rule
A museum is the place for rods of iron.

A child brought up in love will grow in confidence
Be proud, but let them choose their lives.
Don't relive your missed chances through their time
Let their own talents be your guide
To help them reach potential.

To bring up children's not an easy task
Each age brings new impediments
Each phase will pass, overtaken by another
Yet though each stage has worries, all things pass.

Let parents realise the joy of seeing children scatter
To pick up new threads, create their own bright future
And knowing deep inside a tie that binds
In love that stretches on forever
And in their thoughts, though miles may separate you
you always will return.

Myra Christie

THE ROSE GARDEN

My dad has died - and yet I have him still,
The blood-red rose, he so loved half uncurled,
Imparts to me the joy of heaven unseen,
Its depth of beauty takes me to his love,
Which lives beyond God's temporary screen.

He is there in the heart of the yellow rose,
Which gently unfolds in the summer sun,
Beaming its radiance into the day.
And surely, amid the profusion of pink,
His gentle spirit smiles, and says, from each glad rose,
'My love is here'.

In the evening, when the moonlight comes,
I view God's masterpiece again.
The white rose, in its splendour, gleams and glows,
Breathing a peace and purity which transcends my understanding.
And all of heaven seems to be there then.
Surely, for this brief moment, I have glimpsed another plain.
God has used His rose to join my dad and me again.

Brenda Munday

THE TRAMP

In a street in the city
A man approaches me
      Clothes are rags
      Hair like straw
Face is dirty hands are sore
Searching in bins are his job
For a crust and bits and bobs
He has no family or no friends
      All he has is shakes and bends
In his eyes there is a sad story
      He once had pride and dignity
Now all he has is the price
      Of a cup of tea and a slice
      Of bread the following
      Week he was dead.

M Wain

LIFE WITH FEAR

Life is such a wonderful thing
So why do we live in fear?
We can't walk the streets alone
Frightened of what might appear.

You don't seem to feel safe
Wherever you may be
Afraid of everyday dangers
And who or what you might see

When my child grows up in this world
I hope that she doesn't think
That it is OK for people
To take drugs or to turn to drink.

'Cause however hard I try
I can't make her close her eyes
To everyday crimes that surround her
The deceit, dishonesty and lies.

I don't believe that everyone is bad
And that everyone's not good
But there are people who really care
And would change this world if they could.

I do believe you should enjoy your life
But be careful whatever you do
Don't take any risks or cause any grief
Then God might look after you.

Louise Reynolds

ANGUISH

I am dead
My feelings are none.
I take my orders from the elements
and offer no resistance,
Come and see for yourself.
Strike and see no startled eye,
Bite and feel no clenching grasp.
Too long a plaything of love,
My loneliness complete.
My future scarred,
My endlessness secured.
Free from me this weight of persecution.
Forsake even vanity and guide me through this toil.
Help me, please help me . . .

Kevin Smith

EASTER

'Erect the cross' the Roman soldier cried -
Like countless times before, the men complied.
But this was different, they were to find
For he had uttered not a word unkind.
This painful climax to a Christmas morn
Three and thirty years after He was born.
Now humanity exults in tribute rare
That such a man could all our troubles bear.
And in the process, make our night to day,
And peace on earth to contrite heart will stay.
With ever the promise mid our mortal strife
Of fruitful days before eternal life.
And 'it is finished' saw new hope begin,
For those weighed down with black and hideous sin.

Francis A Scollin

FEIGNED MAGIC OF THE FAIR

The fair, a turmoil of pungent smoky smells,
a place of feigned magic.
Where prime coloured lights flash laboriously and
mindlessly.
With all the painful fears of life, replaced and put
aside, only to obtain a fear where no one is really
scared, and the final end is only to step off and
go again.
While the over imaginative, holler fake and
ambitious screams.
The real scream of fear and terror, is lost amongst
the pungent smells, the nauseating traffic of speeding
carriages, and the broad, almost disillusioning lights
of the fair.
Though the one who begs, pleads and only desires
silence, is gradually weakened by the heavy load
put upon the far from strong and guilty body.
No one hears, everyone is blind.
No one hears what real terror is, only the terror
they can control.
But night is in its prime, and it is silent now.
The once bellowing mortal, is far from able to
scream, and left the fair at the same time as
everyone else, but through a much different
exit.

Zita Stockbridge (13)

EXBRIDGE

Devoid of function it laconically stands,
Taking nothing to nowhere and back again.
And as it useless sentry keeps
It remembers the pride at its birth and weeps
Rainwater tears.

Mouth open wide in disbelief
Retirement brought no sweet relief.
The tracks on its head have all but receded
Its function in life is not to be needed,
By man evermore.

A link in the chain till the half century died,
Now a charm on the bracelet of waste countrywide.
It gave up nothing of its own volition
And now has no plans save demolition
At last.

Dean Smirthwaite

WESTON, MY HOME

The sands, the winds, the gulls, the sea,
Weston will always be home to me,
Walking along the sandy shore,
With seaweed, rubbish and gulls galore,
They wheel overhead with a screech and cry,
The town has changed and I wonder why,
Close at hand there is country too
Sadly the sea will never be blue,
Looking at water and the far off lands,
Then back along that stretch of sands,
You will always find the donkeys there
Gazing forlorn and without a care,
Boats in the harbour there are but a few,
Awaiting season and their hardy crew,
Sailing out and around the bay,
With setting sun that's the end of a day,
There's quite a lot left for one to do
And the woods still yet to roam,
It may have changed somewhat today,
But Weston is still my home.

R Ellis

THE SHARING NEED

To share is to give and without so doing,
Then what kind of a life would you be living?
So that is why with someone you share your life
Be it a lover, a husband or a wife.
Be it a friend or a relative,
The object is the same, to take and to give.
For nature herself has designed it to be so,
To love is to share with someone you know.
So with your family you share a home,
Or your life be lonely living alone
You live your life for your family,
A load of responsibilities is what you carry.
It is a life of love and care,
Inspired by the many things you share.
Your problems, your worries, your ups and downs,
The joys and the sorrows of rights and wrongs.
The smiles, the laughs and the quarrels,
The foul smells and your used bath towels.
The shower with your lover
And your dirty bath water.
Your tie and your shoes,
Your cigarettes and your booze.
Your comb, your toothpaste and pyjamas
Your book and your pen, whatever you have,
Even the aggravations of your bad manners.
Your thoughts, your dreams, your entire feelings,
When they are shared, that's when life is
worth living.

N Phillip

LEAVING HOME

It takes more than a day to leave home.
You may walk out the door
and be out of sight
but see!
The feet trudge back along
the old familiar path
without thinking.

It takes more than a week to leave home.
You may have packed a case
and caught a ship, a plane
but still you get homesick
and yearn for the old familiar ways
without realising.

It takes more than a year to leave home.
You may have stormed out,
thrown away the key
and vowed never to return
but all it takes is a frugal time,
a quiet moment
and there you are, back again
turning up like an old penny.

It takes more than a lifetime to leave home.
You may think you are free,
independent at last
but you open your mouth and hear your mother speak,
or help a friend and recognise your father's ways.
Everything new and yours
are just the old familiar patterns
in thin disguise.

Home is the loving beginning.
Home is the loving end.

S E Hutchings

WOULD IT WERE ONLY THE LEAVES THAT ARE DYING

Autumn is misty, winter defying,
Russet the leaves falling and lying,
Summer's green leaves fading and dying.

Humanity rolls with the earth in its season,
Strife and distrust refuting all reason,
Selfish indulgence, smug and uncaring,
Millions in need, distressed and despairing,
Lives of the innocent there for the taking,
Morals and codes so many forsaking,
Unbridled lusts in uncaring style,
False standards of life that only defile.
Nations of power, high standards of living,
Millions more shower, millions more giving
To building the arms, Satanic, prolific,
Weapons of war obscene and horrific.

In primitive lands, bereft of all power,
Disease and starvation, till death calls the hour.

Violence unchained stalks unabated,
Virtue profaned, young lives desecrated.
Gone the clear patterns we cherished of old,
All of the concepts to treasure and hold.

Voice of humanity, caught in the wind sighing,
Would it were only the leaves that are dying.

John A Gilroy

POISON

Black blood runs through her body
her hair as dark as a raven's eyes
A beautiful sight for all to see
from a distant land she awakes

lips as red as a ruby crystal
her touch as cold as ice
she cares for nothing and no one
A beauty for all time
but you can't see or touch her
for she is nothing but a demon in my mind

Emma Brackenbury

THE FUTURE

When you look into the future what do you see?
Do you see happiness - do you see me?
Will I have children will I make my mum a grandma,
Will she be giving her grandchildren sweets, making them say 'ta'.
Will I have a husband who will be a nice man,
Or will I live alone as I cook my tea in the pan?
If I get married will my dad be happy,
Will he babysit his grandchildren and change the dirty nappy?
Will I grow up to be a good nurse,
Or will I be an old lady who likes to curse?
Will I be a coward or will I be brave,
Will I smile at the old lady who will always wave?
Will I be someone who will be very happy,
Or will I be mean, moody and snappy?
Will I still support the blue and whites,
Or will I be watching those boxing fights?
I don't know what will happen to me in my future life,
Will I live alone or be a man's darling wife?
Nobody can read the future nobody knows what will happen,
Will I follow the same routine
Will I go through the same pattern?
I don't want to look into the future
I want to live day by day.
I really don't want to mess up my life in any big way.

I don't know what the future holds for me . . .

Heather Clark (17)

THE LIGHTS OF HOME

On the corner of life is a little direction,
I'll meet you there, we make our own decision.
Inner light shines through my bones,
The blood of Celt, to the lights of home.

Meet me here on the islands shoreline,
Reflect, to empty our minds.
Watch the sea in a grandeur of wisdom,
The blood of Gael, to the lights of home.

In the crease of sky is a spark of light,
A small insertion fills the fire inside.
Hold me tight you are not alone,
The blood of living, to the lights of home.

Behind, the sand has washed our tracks,
never feel a need to turn back.
Always somewhere new to roam,
The blood of freedom, to the lights of home.

Bob Storm

POLLUTION ALLEY

Combustion engines spouting fumes,
Engines running, tyres squealing
Down pollution alley.
Traffic passing by oblivious,
Bumper to bumper, nose to tail
Down pollution alley.

Travelling by road, burning up,
At traffic lights, stop, starting
Down pollution alley.
Stifled breathing of clogged air,
No time to stand and stare
Down pollution alley.

J J D Selby

THOUSANDS ARE STILL ASLEEP

Thousands are still asleep not I my friend
For sleep will not come to me
I lie awake with vacant stare
And reach to touch but you're not there
I hold my breath in case you come
To touch me once again
I dare not fall asleep
In case I miss you

Thousands are still asleep not I my love
An icy hand touches my heart
I'm icy cold now we're apart
I long to feel your lips on mine
But chill is all around

Thousands are still asleep not I
My hunger keeps me awake
No solace can I find
My heart is shrinking in my breast
Where once it burst with love
And I'm alone to yet another dawn

Thousands are still asleep not I the shadow
My soul has gone it left with you
A shell remains, a shell that cannot rest
And never will I know again the shelter of your arms.

Thousands are still asleep not I
Denied all peace since you have gone from me.

Myra Canning

THE NIGHT SHOW

The darkness of the night has fallen, the sky is set for a show,
As one by one the cast appears, to delight the earth below,
First the moon in all its glory, dressed over all with light,
Tries to outshine the rest of the cast, as they appear throughout the night.
A sparkling backdrop as each star arrives, like tiny sequins so bright,
A hush descends across the land, as the moon lights up all in sight,
A soft breeze blows a melody, as the overture begins,
Creatures and animals watch and wait, and somewhere a lonely bird sings,
Now the dawn chorus bursts into song, the stars of the night slip away,
All is bathed in daylight again, until the end of another day.

Penny Rose

TOUCH

Going to bed is what I like
To feel the warm sheets
On such a cold night.
As I slide down the bed
I feel the warmth coming through.
This lovely hot water bottle
Was long overdue.
As I lay in my bed
Ready for sleep
I think of the homeless
Their boxes they keep
How cold they must feel
As the dampness sets in.
Their bones will g row old
Their bodies so thin.
No comfort, or touch
Of warm blankets for them.
 I hope God will guide them
To find love once again.

D M Clancy

SEDUCTION

Winter's cold kiss that chilled our cheek is leaving slow
And now, up these stag-steep slopes of pine
Massed slabs of cloud rise and fly
And shine like freshly-banked grave-chalk
Chime in the eye like birdsong in the rain-freshed, clearing spring sky

Linger awhile in these warming, heathering hills of slumber
Kiss the sun-soaked stones, and day-dreaming among them
I will reel such a world past your heavy head
That all my wise-craft woven words will conspire an enchantment
A sea-change in mind, flower-foaming, blossom-deep, to froth you under

(And my desires
Steeped and simmering through starling-deep, star-stirred black billows
Will turn and rise past you, bubbling, shoaling in the green sea
The hissing raw air to embrace
To swallow you with their massed intensity
And making of your pearl-form a cipher, an object, empty-carapaced

For what is it we all want
But power or a meaning of some sort?
And even satisfied
As we look before us will stretch a new desire's cavernous depths
And beyond that, the next, and the next
But even this knowledge will not stay our hands from grasping
Nor our eyes from these hollows lift)

And I will wet you and cover your spit-spiced lips with mine
And among the fern fronds unfurl your feathered will
Ascending kite-like high over a hundred hills
Into luminous lark-light heaven
Smiling, you will kiss me a thousand times
And not think it one time too many

J Wilde

LIFE'S JOURNEY

Across the water's web of light,
I see a future distant but bright,
A babe in arms at its mother's breast;
> Innocent without care,
Life's ahead out there.

The path is rugged, it twists and turns,
The mountains high, the sun that burns,
A long and tedious journey awaits;
> Hard and bare,
Life's ahead out there.

At the mountain's peak, experiences we share,
A moment of joy, a time of despair,
Carrying the burden onward we go;
> It seems so unfair,
Life's ahead out there.

In no time at all we are at journey's end,
It's time to say, 'goodbye my dear friend',
A life has been lived shadowed in darkness;
> But not all sad,
After all - life's not that bad!

Amanda S Holland

FOUND AND LOST

She looked as a familiar memory.
That struck my mind a fruit divine -
That kindled all my longing anonymity
to leave me mystified.

She was I thought a presentation:
of other people - all in her.
My anguish led to admiration of her form,
her voice her hair - that flowed in length;
that spoke with fun that flowered instant
match of sun.

The race to hope had now returned.
My heart was opened, a new beginning -
The future glimmered of hope - but flickered
Finding the time late past her wedding.

David N Grufferty

OASIS

A long, long journey, with the sand
Piled high in dunes along the lonely way.
Too hot by day, too cold by night.
Too dry! Too dry!
Dry skin, dry flesh, dry mouth, dry bone.
No tears to cry.
Weary. Bone weary. Dry, dry - bone weary.
Ahead - perhaps - an oasis.
Oasis! A mirage?
Is it real?
What does it matter? I can feel
The cool, clear water streaming over me!
I bathe, I drink, my drying, dying self
Leaps back to life!
My new-bright self would like to linger here,
But no - go on I must.
This is no place to stay.
But, when the journey's over, I can say
I remember an oasis.

Doreen Fiol

A STERLING RACE

As liquidity drips through my fingers
And I wash my hands of the miseries of my success
I falter for a moment, and consider in a different light
These gleaming globules wrought of lesser mortals
Who by their own deficiencies failed, yet were blameless
Unable to sympathise, I turn in pity
From my reservoir, acknowledge debt
And thus removing the debris of conscience,
Rejoin the human race.

Clare Woodward

NATURE

As I sit here pondering,
Of God's earth, sky and sea.

The white and silver waves cascade,
Upon the rocks.

As the birds,
Swift and agile,
Swoon down upon the sea,
To catch the fish,
And fly off gleefully.

The rain in silver droplets,
Pours down grace upon the earth.

Fishermen with lobster pots,
Earn their daily bread.

Children with bucket and spade,
Make sandcastles in the air.

Mary Porter

DUSK AND DAWN

When dusk meets dawn in a hot loving summer,
The roses die a little, melting scent into sense
For the dance of glow-worms and grasshoppers.
In the cornfields' delicious suicide of hayrolls
All is golden abandon, lush tirade against autumn skies,
Old age and dead romance.

When dusk meets dawn, we take strange steps
To that primitive tune (for the world is ending, burning),
Where sunset scorches the green of the daisy's awakening eye and
We at once are shadows and earth, bone and root,
Hiding in tree hollows,
Making the wood sing.

Time hangs breathless on the boughs where we walk,
And the stars yawn into themselves,
Constant through all our tomorrows.
We squeeze light through our fingers till it pours, liquid gold
Into green and dust - and the seasons become one:
Your years are drowned in me; you are baptised mine, an innocent.

As dawn meets dusk, our fingers touch;
Heart beating, souled mouths meet and we
Hold the world in the concave between two bellies.
Earth waits trembling, the moon watching is peopled, huge witness
To its own extinction as the sun too roars to meet itself,
A cooler fire reborn from the bleeding red: wise, conquered, triumphant.

Soma Ghosh

WAR CHILD

Twisted, broken, mutilated, pained, sunken eyes, whispering
refrain. Tear stained cheeks, sibilant cries, the war child's
life.
Bosnia, Sarajevo, Lebanon, Saigon, endlessly *on and on and
on!*
Bullets through tissue, bombs take no sides, *listen, listen*
as the innocence cries.

When the fighting is over and the conflict's at end, when General
kisses General and foe becomes friend. When memorials are made
to the brave soldiers dead. Then see the children at the war's
end.

Blinded eyes can't see rainbows, nor lost arms lift pots of gold
crippled legs can't give chase, deaf ears can't hear stories
told, tiny souls can't be lifted from six foot dug holes.

Through the rivers of tears, over the misty aeons of time, the
war child has suffered endless war crimes, they take up no arms
they have no defence, they are always the victims, whichever
side the fence.
I see no statues, or plaques in *their* names, for *pity's sake!*
Save . . . the war child!

W T J Saward

HIDE ME FROM THE REAL WORLD

Hide me from the real world
But where are all the real people?
I don't care for minor distractions
Contractions, subtractions, devotions and lotions
Celebrities from MT-3
The world where fame is cheap
Everybody has nobody
They need someone, but they can't see it
But I can't either, but I don't care

Hide my fear from those with power
I'll wield my gun before the end
The day will fade to night I fear
And night will fade to day
This will never go away
Maybe time will show the answers
Maybe no-one knows the questions
We'll stand together when the time comes
I feel apart from anything, everything
I feel alone when I close my eyes
I am alone when I open them

Hide me from the real world
Shelter my mind from the real despair
People suffering in the endless war
Wondering what we all live for
Wondering if it will ever end

Derry Wootton

THE MOON

The full moon shone down in its autumn whisper, its misted shroud enveloping it like a secret aura, as a sudden breeze whisked the clouds from the moon's face, it stared down at me as if transfixing time. The frosted glaze left in its wake showering negative beams down onto the dewless carpet of wilderness leaving nothing but the whispering eddies of the late day's warmth.

Fiona Fuller

JUST MY JEAN

When she smiles it brightens my day
And then the dark clouds drift away
But if she's sad and feeling blue
I simply don't know what to do

We've been together so many years
Had our laughter, shed some tears
Her brow is furrowed, her hair is grey
But my love for her is there to stay

In our garden, with veg and flowers
We spend so many happy hours
We like our walks and dances too
There always is so much to do

And when at last the day is done
It's just my Jean, the only one

G W Goodban

CHARLOTTE

The blue leather shoes, scuffed at the toes,
Are pulled from the cupboard so I can pose.
A red floppy cardigan borrowed from sis
Acts as a dress this is just bliss.
I've combed my hair and altered my looks
Added colour to my lips and some to my books.

Now! In this toy cupboard I saw a hat.
Open the door and torment the cat.
Where's that bonnet, let's take a good look.
Oh dear my phone's been left off the hook.
And I've found a handbag with a broken catch.
Stuffed inside is my doll with a patch.

Right at the back, it must be there.
Oh look, half a bickie for me and teddy to share.
Red plastic cup, some orange squash.
How lovely this is, isn't it posh.
There in the cupboard I can just about see
The hat which granny gave to me.

Come now teddy you must have a drink
Then I'll wash you in the kitchen sink.
The hat looks kind of grubby too
So I'll pop it in the wash with you.
Hey, mummy is calling, I must go and see.
Oh goody it's time for me to have tea.

Marlene Tapscott

EDWARD THOMAS - A LETTER HOME

The oak shifts its weight of leaves
Like a rusty suit of armour.
An owl shivers.
Somewhere in the distance
The terrible, bitter cries
Of dog-fox and vixen -
Greek ululations
Across moon-silvered English woods.
Everywhere, the sweet stealthy stench
Of putrefaction and decay -
How old the world is -
How sinister and innocent.
All this so that the earth,
As Lazarus was commanded, stumbles painfully
Towards the raw dawn
And transfiguration -
Green and white, blue and gold -
While in the east
Night combs the stars from her hair.

Dorothy Ireland

LONGING

Where the minnows dart and leap,
Where there's fields of grazing sheep,

Where there's corn and purple heather,
Where the wild bird picks her feather,

That's the place I long to be,
'Neath the weeping willow tree.

Where starry streams flow tinkling by,
To shine therein the heron's eye,

Where sunlight darts between the stones,
to paint the spray with his bright tones,

Where otters hunt the deep cool pools,
and gentle mother nature rules.

What lovelier place than this for me,
Beneath the weeping willow tree.

But alas I do but dream,
of darting fish and sparkling stream,

For I am many miles from home,
No more the willow banks to roam,

But these bright memories do I keep,
Through wakeful hours and tranquil sleep
and always in my thoughts I'll be,
Beneath that weeping willow tree.

Ken Jones

SLOW-TIME CAFE

This fishbowl in which I sit, stands still,
Motionless in time, its occupants sit and ponder,
A respite from the outside stresses of life.
'Ants' scitter and scamper past the glass,
Oblivious to the on-lookers, they continue
On their, 'oh so important' missions.
Male, female, young and old, merge and
Blur, as they hurry on past.

Some, preened to perfection, stride out,
Bursting with confidence, they 'own' the world.
Their 'designer skins' glint in the sunlight,
Dazzling the aspiring translators with images and labels of power.
Others, locked in grim determination, stride past,
Conscious only of their inner struggles with reality.
Oblivious to all around them, they march on,
Between the parting waves of human interruptions.

Irritation appears to flood around the glass,
Sweeping in from all directions, yet unable to come through,
It passes on, soaking all that get in its way.
In this haven, this sanctuary against all the modern,
Human conditioning of 'faster, quicker . . . *now*',
We sit, separately from each other, yet huddled together,
All with the singular purpose of rest and pause.

Infrequently, stressed out urbanites break away,
From the steady march of 'progress'.
They slip through the glass, its surface healing behind them.
For them, there is but a short time to acclimatise,
As they order for their bodily need,
A conscious, rather than instinctive choice,
Then, *time* washes away, to leave peace and relaxation.

Richard B Sharples

WHO AM I?

Who am I?
Quiet and shy, noisy and loud
Brave, independent, weak or a coward
Quick to change temper, slow to regret
Shadow in the corner forgotten once met.
Evil troublemaker, founder of peace
Full of advice yet eager to please
Never quite right, never quite wrong
Never to hear when praises are sung.
Used and discarded, grumble or grouse
To rage in a temper or be quiet as a mouse
Predictable sometimes, a little too sane
Steps over the mark, the person to blame.
Always the villain, sometimes the good
Trying to do things the way that I should
Smiles and tears, joy and dismay
Lonely, depressed, yet happy next day.
So now when I question,
Who really am I?
A jumble of this
That's who am I!

Gill Price

MYSTIC LOVER

In indigo hours where formless forms abound,
And with angelic forces there,
You come to me and hold my heart
And touch my soul, and care.

Reaching down inside of me you say
I'm part of you, and all else too.
You blend and merge my spirit till
I know not if I'm me or you.

Or if we'll ever meet in flesh, to touch
The sun, the moon and stars, to hold
And love so much, we two, as one
Forever until time grows old.

Or are you just a cosmic dream of dust
That flees before the song of lark.
Tonight please stay, though dawn creeps in,
My mystic lover of the dark.

Irene Carss

DAD

I remember him well, broad, strong and muscular
Yet he was a gentle giant.
he stood 6ft tall, no taller, no smaller,
Just 6ft - that's all.
Hands like a digging machine,
Always soft, always gentle - always clean.
He worked hard to earn his pay,
That we might have food and clothing every day.
I remember him that way.
He was strict and his justice sure,
Sometimes I didn't like that but I knew it was the right cure.
Look after us he would, whether we were bad or good.
When we were ill, his love he'd give
Till we'd had our fill.
I remember him well that way.
When he left us for that mansion in the sky,
I found I couldn't cry and I always wondered why?
I really miss you dad.

T J Lucas

THE SCHOOL REGISTER OF THE THIRTIES

Miss Devlin, class three teacher
Carried her register like a preacher
And placed it neatly on her table,
Opened it, sat down; she was able
To see us all from her vantage point . . .
. . . She was thin and angular, every joint
Was sharp, like the eyes in her head,
Which at times filled you with a sort of dread.
'Now, are we all here?' she would sharply ask
While we young children assumed our mask
Of total obedience; 'Yes, Miss Devlin' we would say
To the name that was aimed our way.
'Amy Bridges?' she called twice, and loud,
No one answered from that obedient crowd,
'Does anyone know why she is not here today?'
One red-haired girl, eager to please, did say,
'She's gone to Carlisle Miss, by train, for the day.
'Cos there's a special trip on Mondays in May'.
When all names were checked, not once, but twice . . .
Miss Devlin gave us a lecture on having head lice!
'There is an inspection next week by the nurse,
So get your hair washed and combed', her terse
Voice echoed throughout that infant class,
Then we were sent out for drill . . . en masse.

E Monaghan

MY FRIEND

On a visit to the churchyard
Where lay my mam and dad
I met a man at a graveside
Whom I'd known as a lad

We spoke of days gone by
Fond memories we could share
Of friends we had known
Who were now lying there

We met again in the village
And many times we talked
Of how the place had changed
And the places we had walked

Then for some time I did not meet him
What was wrong, I could not tell
Until a friend told me the reason
He said, 'He is not well'

I promised that I would visit
When next his house I passed
But promises are broken
And then I called at last

I chatted with my friend that day
And then bade him goodbye
I'm pleased I went to see my friend
That night he passed away

Norman Rayne

UNTITLED

I like you for your gentle way
The sweetness of the things you say
So softly in your words to me
With tenderness I feel, and see
A person who is nice to be with
When alone I feel so shy
You're friendly, but you never pry
Into my deepest thoughts I conceal
The need in me, for you, I feel
So happy when you come to share
Your thoughts with me, you scare me
In the way you make me
More and more and more
Just lately,
Love you.

Lesley Marie Hewett

SKY

The limitless limit that bounds our sight
By day, and brightens the dark of night
Has seen all nature live and die,
Has watched brave creatures try to fly
Beyond the blue, from Newton's grip
Their fiery tails and bold heads slip
But only now does Sky see them reach
And upward soar, herself to breach.

She sees us all below, and their pretence
At her protection, her defence
She knows their folly - for it is in vain
That they still try to relieve her pain
And she is wise, and all-forgiving
Of the transience of the living
But even she can't tell if man
Really is the last part of the plan.

Sky's beauty is in her changing face
As across the sun and moon do chase
Not quite for ever - for despite the bold
Appearance she knows she will grow old
And after Venus, but before warlike Mars
She will meet her sisters in the stars
But for now she contents herself to hear
The roaring giants rise above her sphere.

But as those creatures thrust and heave
Sky's turbulent atmosphere to leave
Into the silence of the other half
They know not when or where their path
Does take them, but trust in their strong soul
For fate will only hint at their goal
Until they know the dawn does rise
On millions of other, younger Skies.

Richard Dawson

UNTITLED

Twisted vision
Disguises perfect views
As emotional fires
Singe lungs of strangers.
Rain tumbles to mask
Brilliant sunshine
And extinguish forgotten dreams
So their existence is no longer possible.
Words turn to water
From water to vapour
That rises to the sunbeams
And plays with the stars.

L K Tiplady

THE LAKE

Sitting beside the lake,
and sheltering from the light drizzle of rain,
beneath the outstretched branches,
of a leafy tree,

As I stare in front of me at the wide expanse
of water,
I see that it's surface is as shiny and clear as
a sheet of glass,
only being broken by indentations,
of gentle drops of rain,

Above, the sky is pale blue, grey,
a raindrop drips from a leaf and splashes onto
my notepad as I write this poem,
it runs across the paper like a tear of happiness,

For happy is how I feel right now,
as I take in the peace and tranquillity of my surroundings
for there is nothing as beautiful,
as the scenes of nature,

Across the lake an angler sits on his seat box,
beneath the nylon confines of a huge umbrella,
I can see the steam rising from the hot drink,
that he cups in his hands,

The quacking of ducks permeates the air,
communicating as they glide across the lakes surface
and birds in the trees around me,
chirp and sing in harmony,

It's at times like this,
that I appreciate the world,
and feel total peace,
within myself.

Paul Warwick

LIKE SOMEONE IN LOVE . . .

When your hands, my love,
reach out towards me,
why do they hesitate?
I can assure you that I long to feel
your hands caressing
the softness of my skin.
Please, my love,
feel the warmth that lies
here at my breast.
Observe, my love, the beating
that you have placed in my heart
Explore me with all your hands,
I will not resist.
I am yours, and only yours,
and I beg you not to doubt me.
All the years of my life
I have been in search of your touch,
and it feels, my sweet,
like someone in love.

My love, if you do not have a voice
with which to speak,
then take my voice.
And if you cannot find the words to say,
then use my words.
They are 'I love you!'
Three simple words,
so easy to say,
so hard to forget.

Alistair Chattaway

NO LAUGHING MATTER

The fears they cannot face,
too hurtful to recall the cause.
Frightened to sleep, afraid of the day,
of sudden light and opening doors.

The choking terror, being held down,
that wish they could just die.
Longing for love and affection,
trust in someone's eye.

Sudden blinding light shatters safety of night,
harsh voice, terror again comes to smother.
The longing to run and hide away
from the cruel deceit of another.

The torment that someone they trusted,
looked up to, for truth and care,
has betrayed them and soiled them,
hurt them and spoiled them,
when tempted into kindness's lair.

Now that they're older
they still have bad scars,
things make them too angry or mild,
visions flash them back or some harsh word,
again they're the tortured child.

They cannot enjoy life as others,
join in the fun others have.
They can smile and smirk,
but it doesn't really work.
These quiet ones have no real laugh.

T P Bradley

UNTITLED

I would like a neat house
Painted green and white
with a neat white fence around

Warm sunshine all the year
Not a sound
But children laughing

A little stream
to sparkle softly
over many coloured pebbles

Some trees with leaves
To catch the wind
And birds to perch in them

An avenue
where I could walk
to find you there
Full of magic light
and our laughter
and I would always
find you there.

A Sander

YOU MUST CONTAIN THE FOUNDATIONS

It is perceived wisely
Words of inspiration
A view of natural phenomenon
For undivided concentration.

The subjects can vary
Consisting of intriguing philosophy
Intelligence is a factor
Or supernatural telepathy.

Seriously what a genius signifies
Is nectar honey to the bee
In Greek mythology a drink of the gods
Is that just a fallacy.

What is an enormous advantage
Referring to a stimulant
It is not always temporarily but accelerates
Love when brilliant.

The poet laureate
Is smothered in exalted delight
For his celestial compositions
Which are addictive and excite.

Shane Jason

THE TREASURE OF COUNTY DOWN

There's a quaint little village called Groomsport
it's the treasure of County Down
the beautiful natural unspoilt views
are where its riches are found
Cockle Row Cottage with thatched roof made by hand
all species of birds on Cockle Island
Bally McCormick Point round to Ballyholme
is a walk you'll remember long after you're home
Orlock is going towards Donaghadee
in the Groomsport House you can have high tea
There are picnic tables or seats just to rest
to enjoy the view or whatever you think best
fishing from harbour attracts mostly boys
men like the boats the big boys' toys
Ladies like to walk or just lay on the beach
so long as the kiddies stay within reach
children play in the sand with their bucket and spade
then off to the water and in they wade
they have so much fun you can guess by their yells
and before they go home they shall gather shells
toddlers love the paddling pool, grandparents watch
from the shade to keep cool
Tennis courts house, those that feel fit
locals watch from their windows as they sip tea or knit
As you can see Groomsport caters for all
so why not come and give Groomsport a call
it's a visit you're sure to remember
should you come January or December.

Joan Lampard

SPRINGTIME

I like the sound of
Springtime
And the birds in the treetops
Singing their song of love.
The stillness of the trees
As it whistles through
The breeze.
Not a cloud in the sky
I see patience flowing
By.
'Cause, I love the sound
Of springtime.
That breeze is in the air
And flowers budding their
Blossom.
At that time of year.

Rodger Nuttall

THIS LIFE

Sweet perfume from the meadows, enveloped in the early dew.
The birds awake and sing their song, as the sun comes shining through,
Warming all upon the earth, giving life and strength anew.

New babes are born this lovely day; they too are part of God's great plan.
We love, and tend their every need, protecting them as best we can.
Alas! One day these babes will grow - the truth about this world to know.

Our creator planned this world, desiring it be filled with love.
But hate and evil took command - so strong, they cannot be removed.
Yes, the sun still shines, and the birds still sing, but the peace
                                                          of long ago - is lost.

The bomb's smoke now obliterates the sun; the noise drowns
                                            the singing of the birds.
Instead, the sound of wailing comes, from ambulances, and injured innocents.
Our main ambition must surely be - to restore our world to sanity.

Then, once again, life will be sweet, united all, we'll happy be.
With joy and love within our hearts - the world will ring with harmony.
When the evil, man made things are gone, we'll live forever in the sun.

Jean Platt

CULLODEN MOOR . . .

Standing on Culloden Moor, the air so still,
my soul acquires an eerie chill, many years
past from that fateful day, but the vision of
death is here to stay . . .
The Highland people stood their ground as the
English horde did gather round. The tartan line
began to charge, but the cannonballs ceased
their bravely march, killing and maiming all
in their path, spewing carnage like Satan's wrath.
The Highland brave fell down like rain in oh
such agony and pain. Now Bonnie Prince Charlie's
dream was gone, the English turned, their job
was done . . .
Amidst the blood-soaked heather, lay generations
lost forever. Men and women in their prime,
cut down like wheat at harvest time, and
Highland clans from distant glens will never
see their homes again, their spirits wander
the shadows of time, through misty glen and
mountainside . . .

Andrew Usher

HUSBAND TO WIFE

Like a soft-breathing statue in marbling moonlight,
Half shrouded by coverlet drapery.
Her body, small, perfect,
And as cold as under-sea stone.

I turn, brush a leg over hers,
Caress her softly.
Her heart beats faster
Like mine,
But as my body grows hot,
Tingle-aching with the feel of her -
Her smooth, baby-skin;
The smell of her, all Chanel and shampoo,
Hers is cold.
As her breathing grows faster and audible
Her body turns
Away and not towards.

She is a foetus:
A see-through blue moonlight embryo
Closed in upon itself,
Knowing only its own comfort,
Not wishing to be touched, pulled,
Brought out and handled.
Her lips partly open,
Her breath like the ocean -
A shell to my ear.
Her eyes too tightly closed for real sleep.

Johanna S Emeney

CONSCIENCE

A hand reaches out from the void
Clutching, grasping at air.
Swathed in mist, it
Plucks at nothing
Just a hand.
Solitary.
Pained it beckons
Help?
A fist
Clenched.
I run - afraid; haunted
Of what I have not yet seen.
Yet,
I turn; *slowly*
Now knowing of what I am frightened.
With howling swirls
The blackness shrivels from view
The hand . . .

Gone

Susie Crozier

MEMORIES

The scent of blossom in the air, stirs memories
    in my mind.
They take me back to childhood days, when peace
    and happiness were the password of mankind.
It seems as though my thoughts project, pictures
    on a screen
And I see trees, distant hills and fields of
    shaded green -
Where early morning mists roll silently
    along the ground
As the clamour of the birds in song awakes -
- The earth at dawn, greeting a new day with
    a joyous sound.

Weak pale rays of sunshine, struggled to pierce
    the hazy sky,
As we ran barefoot through the dewy grass
    to chase a butterfly.
Soft warm breezes caress our face, bringing
    colour to the cheek
Whilst we played our childhood games, of *tag*
    or *hide and seek*.
Maybe some days we would just sit and dream
Or pick the wild flowers from the bank of a
    gently flowing stream.
Often the droning of a busy bee. Disturbed
    the peace of day
As we lay content beneath a shady tree, savouring
    the warm sweet smell of hay.
Oh! Those happy youthful days without a
    doubt or care!
These things I remember, when the scent
    of blossoms fill the air.

C Worthington

HIS WORDS

Once there lived a man
a prophet was he
who claimed to see the future
and didn't like
what he did see.
Through blood, death and fire
the world we live in today
will one day come to an end.
With starvation, drought and great light
was the message, he did try to send.
Can we understand this man,
or will we ever
and will his words last forever
he'd seen what will come of us
that man called Nostradamus.
Though man will survive
another world another side
through space we'll ride.
Should we believe
what will come of us
the words of Nostradamus.

Darren Sidney

INFORMATION

We hope you have enjoyed reading this book - and that you will continue to enjoy it in the coming years.

If you like reading and writing poetry drop us a line, or give us a call, and we'll send you a free information pack.

Write to

>Anchor Books Information
>1-2 Wainman Road
>Woodston
>Peterborough
>PE2 7BU